Accidental Sabbatical

Hope for Surviving and Thriving While Unemployed

By Shari Risoff

ACCIDENTAL SABBATICAL
Hope for Surviving and Thriving While Unemployed
2nd Edition

Project Mavens
Raleigh, NC
projectmavens@risoff.com
https://accidentalsabbatical.wordpress.com/

ISBN 978-0-9911433-2-0 (paperback)
ISBN 978-0-9911433-3-7 (ebook)

Scripture quotations taken from *The Holy Bible: New Living Translation (NLT)*. Carol Stream: Tyndale House Publishers, 1996, 2004, 2007 unless otherwise noted.

Acknowledgements

For Stephen, my soul mate, my love, and a constant source of positive energy in my life. Our hope is in the Lord as we travel this journey together. Without Stephen's unconditional support and encouragement, I would most likely be whining and not writing.

Thank you to Brian Godawa, for a brilliant cover design. Thank you to my beta readers, Dayna, Teri, Phyllis, Danielle, Michael, Kim, Arlene, Darrel and Shelley, some employed, some not, all of whom provided valuable feedback and insight.

And most of all I thank the Almighty God who has given me a part to play in his story... May this bring glory and honor to him.

CONTENTS

Prologue

When my husband accepted a new position across country, I resigned my job, choosing to become the "trailing spouse" rather than live more than 1000 miles apart. Although I knew the job market had disintegrated I didn't think it would be a problem to find a new job, having a great track record and references. So I took a month off after my job ended to settle into my new state and this new season. It turned out to be more difficult than I expected. One month became two, then three, then the difficult milestone of a year.

It had become an Accidental Sabbatical.

It just doesn't seem to end. At least it hasn't ended for me yet and it has been longer than the traditional sabbatical year.

As each month passes, I dutifully do everything I am supposed to do and yet still receive no offer. And I am not alone; I have met many others traveling the same roads. Through it all, I have never regretted the decision to choose my marriage over a paycheck.

On a Saddleback Church broadcast, I heard Kay Warren speak about her Hope Box; a collection of verses that the Lord had given her over the years to provide hope. She wrote them on index cards and kept them in a little box. I immediately started my own Hope Box, scribbling scriptures and inspirational thoughts on the cards right then. They help me focus and breathe.

I want to do more than just survive this Accidental Sabbatical. I want to thrive in it and to arrive whole and improved from the process. I am adjusting to this new life, figuring out how to *be* and what to *do* during this season.

My goal in writing this book is to inspire with these things:

1. Thoughts of hope I have found through Scripture and authors who have impacted me.

2. Personal examples of my own discovery of hope in the midst of this Accidental Sabbatical.

3. A short written exercise to help actively apply and practice hope, despite feelings.

I encourage you to create a Hope Box... it will help you look for hope. As you read these words of encouragement and hope I pray they will help you too.

I considered waiting until I had a job to finish this book, to provide the perfect happy ending we all want. But the point is to have hope no matter where you are in the journey. So where it says 'The End', it is really *To Be Continued...*

* * *

Chapter 1: Hope

- - - - - - - - - - - - - - - - - -

Jeremiah 29:11
For I know the plans I have for you, declares the Lord,
plans to prosper you and not to harm you, plans to
give you hope and a future.

- - - - - - - - - - - - - - - - -

There are millions of us on an Accidental Sabbatical, unemployed and searching a job. For some of us this is a search for significance; for others, simply a search for a paycheck and for most of us, probably both.

One woman asked me, 'Why aren't you livid? Why talk about hope instead of revenge?' Her question surprised me, because it made me realize I am not holding on to anger or seeking revenge. What would be the point? Another friend said the opposite: 'I'm so tired of hearing job horror stories. I want to know there is hope! There is hope, right?'

Yes! I choose to focus on hope instead of anger or depression and when I do, negative emotions disappear.

J.T. O'Donnell, founder of Careerealism.com, addressed the emotional side of sudden unemployment in a webinar, and here is a summary: *Process all of the emotions that come with a job loss. Allow yourself to have a pity party for 24-48 hours. Grieve the loss of your job, feel the anger, and the fear of what will change and what's to come. Then you're done and you move on.*

My 48 hour pity party ended long ago.

This is a season and every season changes.

This is a season of hope.

— — — — — — — — — — — — — — — — — — — —

Hope begins in the dark, the stubborn hope that if you just show up and try to do the right thing, the dawn will come. You wait and watch and work: you don't give up.

~ Anne Lamott[i]

— — — — — — — — — — — — — — — — — — — —

So I head out to the Monday morning job seeker group meeting at the church. Something about these meetings being held in a church building comforts me. On one side of the room, eight foot tables are set up, three in a row. Two volunteers stand behind each table, handing out blank nametags and a blue Sharpie and say, "Write your name and area of expertise on your badge." One woman is having us log in on an attendance list and another hands out flyers, announcing today's breakout sessions.

Some Mondays the small groups break into job category groups, where all sales and marketing people meet in one room, human resources in another, etc. Other days there are function-specific sessions, such as role-playing for interviews or resume clinics and sometimes a special speaker.

On the other side of the room is the coffee table and everywhere in between are the job seekers. The room is packed, men and women of all ages, dressed in business attire, hoping to network their way to a new job.

Much like a grief recovery meeting, people are in different stages of acceptance. Some people are actually relieved that they are unemployed, having voluntarily left a position they did not like. Others are still in shock, having received the proverbial pink slip, and then walked out of the building by the security guard.

At this meeting, most of us make our way to the coffee pot as soon as possible. It gives us something to do next. The coffee cup gives us something to handle and look at while we wait for someone to approach us with an outstretched hand. I try to be the one to break the silence and greet someone, and to get them talking about themselves.

The very first meeting I attended I met Jennifer, who had just resigned from the HR department of a company where I had just applied. After hearing her reasons for leaving, I was not at all disappointed when they did not call me to interview. It was my first sign of hope that God was in it and there would be no coincidences.

All seasons begin and end.

Eventually.

Right?

- -

1 Peter 5:12b
My purpose in writing is to encourage you and assure you that what you are experiencing is truly part of God's grace for you. Stand firm in this grace.

- -

Always remember that your present situation is not your final destination. The best is yet to come.
~ Zig Ziglar

- -

Each of us has a story. You may have been fired by a vindictive manager, or are one of thousands caught in a 'reduction in force' (RIF). Some days are discouraging but other days we are encouraged. No matter what happened, we *have* to have hope to survive. And that hope is **not** the kind of hope that politicians promise because as we all know, that type doesn't last past Election Day.

One thing I know for sure is that my hope is found in Jesus, and in his love for me. I stay encouraged when I focus on him, the source of my hope. He is right here walking beside me in this season. It is a season of hope.

- -

Hope is not what you expect. It is what you would never dream.
~ Max Lucado[ii]

- -

In the book of Ecclesiastes in the Bible there is a list of seasons that are applicable to my Accidental Sabbatical.

Ecclesiastes 3:1-8

For everything there is a season,

a time for every activity under heaven.

A time to be born and a time to die.

A time to plant and a time to harvest.

A time to kill and a time to heal.

A time to tear down and a time to build up.

A time to cry and a time to laugh.

A time to grieve and a time to dance.

A time to scatter stones and a time to gather stones.

A time to embrace and a time to turn away.

A time to search and a time to quit searching.

A time to keep and a time to throw away.

A time to tear and a time to mend.

A time to be quiet and a time to speak.

A time to love and a time to hate.

A time for war and a time for peace.

How many of these seasons have you been through?

It certainly is a time to grieve, and to heal.

We are planting seeds now, and in time we will harvest.

We will keep some things and throw away others. We are definitely searching and ultimately, one day, that will end.

We will learn, stretch and grow.

I choose to believe that everything happens for a reason. Maybe you don't see the reason right now, but when it is finally revealed, it will blow you away.

* * *

Like I often do, you may feel like you are failing your family or yourself and like I have, you may let the fear take over some days. Don't beat yourself up and don't give in to doubt or depression. I know it's easier said than done; that is why it is a daily decision to have a conscious hope.

- -

Philippians 4:19
And this same God who takes care of me will supply all your needs from his glorious riches, which have been given to us in Christ Jesus.

- -

I try not to spread negative emotions anywhere except in my private journal; I only open that bottle in writing or in prayer. Which makes it all the more amazing when an encouraging gift of hope arrives, letting me know God sees me and knows what I feel.

Merriam-webster.com's defines sabbatical:
Sabbatical noun
: a period of time during which someone does not work at his or her regular job and is able to rest, travel, do research, etc.

My sabbatical has definitely been accidental – unintentional, unexpected. Unplanned for sure; I certainly never thought it would be this long.

When my job first ended I looked forward to maybe 30 days of rest, perhaps even a full quarter, because after all, I had just finished five years of hard work with monthly numbers to meet and only periodic one week vacations. So the idea of several weeks off in a row delighted me. I had earned them.

When we moved I was sure I would have no problem finding work in a new state but then months became more than a year, and delight turned to concern, and then to something resembling panic.

In some ways this sabbatical feels like a previous one I chose to take. When my son was born, I chose to be a stay-at-home mom for the first three years of his life. Then when it was evident that he needed to be hanging out with people his own age all day, I went job hunting and quickly found work. It is not that way today. Especially in a depressed job market and when I am no longer in my 20's and no longer an entry level worker.

Now is a much different time; both in my life, and in the global job market. For those of us with multiple degrees and/or multiple years of experience, we find ourselves wondering why we spent the time and money to over-educate and over-qualify ourselves. At least that's how I feel sometimes and I know many others who feel the same way.

We are seasoned, experienced, have multiple skills that would be valuable assets to a company. Yet, nothing.

- -

Deuteronomy 31:8
Do not be afraid or discouraged, for the Lord will personally go ahead of you. He will be with you; he will neither fail you nor abandon you.

- -

I hope to encourage you and to encourage myself to get through this and come out of it unscathed, or at least relatively so.

It feels cliché to hear 'hang in there', or any of the other things people say to offer encouragement. But I visualize the Almighty God personally walking with me, sometimes in front of me, carrying me some days, walking beside me on others, but always with me. Without fail.

Especially on the days when I can't even fake a positive attitude, I close my eyes and just visualize God right here with me.

He is there with you too.

- -

Psalm 121:5-6
The Lord himself watches over you! The Lord stands beside you as your protective shade. The sun will not harm you by day, nor the moon at night.

- -

We are not alone on this journey.

Long-term unemployment has set in for millions of Americans in the past several years. I have more time on my hands than I can ever remember. I don't mind being alone; in fact I am actually quite comfortable being by myself. But I struggle with down time and lack of deadlines. I am a doing kind of person. When I feel there is no end in sight, it hits me that this might be my new reality – this might be *it*. This Accidental Sabbatical may just be permanent retirement without any golden parachute, without choice.

Then doubt sets in. But Zig Ziglar used to say that doubt kills more dreams than failure ever will so when that black cloud of doubt and fear threaten, I fight it with faith.

– – – – – – – – – – – – – – – – – – –

Psalm 39:6-7
We are merely moving shadows, and all our busy rushing ends in nothing. We heap up wealth, not knowing who will spend it. And so, Lord, where do I put my hope? My only hope is in you.

– – – – – – – – – – – – – – – – – – –

Hope combats doubt; just like darkness is eliminated by turning on the light. If this really is a permanent sabbatical, what will I do with the rest of my life? When I dwell on that thought, I fall back into a frenzy of 'doing'. I need to learn how to just be… To be comfortable with myself no matter what.

– – – – – – – – – – – – – – – – – – – –

Relying on God has to begin all over again every day as if nothing had yet been done. ~ C. S. Lewis[iii]

– – – – – – – – – – – – – – – – – – – –

Psalm 33:4-5
For the word of the Lord holds true and we can trust everything He does. He loves whatever is just and good; the unfailing love of the Lord fills the earth.

– – – – – – – – – – – – – – – – – – – –

It is better to have hope than to be without it – of course. But what do we do when we are not feeling hopeful?

How do I move from hopeless to hopeful?

I have to get out of my own head. And then to get out of the house, get out of the rut... go find someone to help, someone to listen to, someone to love. Go sit in a coffee shop; buy someone a cup of coffee.

Get the heart pumping... exercise to a workout video, go swim laps, or run miles. Get moving. Help someone. There are days that I sit still and just 'be'. But some days I must *do* something to stay sane.

– – – – – – – – – – – – – – – – – – – –

Romans 1:12 NCV
Help each other with the faith we have. Your faith will help me, and my faith will help you.

– – – – – – – – – – – – – – – – – – – –

Faith indeed tells what the senses do not tell, but not the contrary of what they see. It is above them and not contrary to them.

~ Pascal[iv]

- - - - - - - - - - - - - - - - - - -

Most of the time it is a lot easier said than done, and those are the times that I have to push myself. Personally, I am a list-maker. Highlighting completed activities on a list makes me feel productive.

So I make a list and start doing things. I read truths from my Hope Box for encouragement. I also:

Read the Bible.

Pray. Out loud. (Whine if necessary but then ask for help and thank God for everything.)

Journal. Write it out.

Listen to music. Sing along.

Dance.

Get. Out. Of. The. House.

Pray for someone to help.

- - - - - - - - - - - - - - - - - - -

I have learned that faith means trusting in advance what will only make sense in reverse.

~ Philip Yancey[v]

- - - - - - - - - - - - - - - - - - -

Isaiah 43:16-19

I am the Lord, who opened a way through the waters, making a dry path through the sea. I called forth the mighty army of Egypt with all its chariots and horses. I drew them beneath the waves, and they drowned, their lives snuffed out like a smoldering candlewick. But forget all that — it is nothing compared to what I am going to do. For I am about to do something new. See, I have already begun! Do you not see it? I will make a pathway through the wilderness. I will create rivers in the dry wasteland.

- -

God says in that verse that he is about to do something new? Well I personally don't see anything new yet. But I am waiting. And I just keep reading my cards in the Hope Box and scriptures. And I wait with expectation and I will be ready when it springs up. Because I am excited to see what the Lord is going to do, and where he will make the pathway for me.

Faith is my sword against the dragon of doubt.

- -

Doubt has a way of magnifying reality into the insurmountable. But faith, well, faith doesn't magnify anything. Rather, it reveals.
~ Timothy Willard[vi]

- -

God is reshaping parts of this clay pot that is my life and my faith is getting stronger as He squeezes and molds me and begins to unfold what He has planned for my life.

The 'big reveal' has yet to happen, but I know it is coming and I am eager to see what He is making of me.

- - - - - - - - - - - - - - - - - - -

Ephesians 2:10
For we are God's masterpiece. He has created us anew in Christ Jesus, so we can do the good things he planned for us long ago.

- - - - - - - - - - - - - - - - - - -

What does He have planned for me during this season of life? I cannot wait to find out!

* * *

Personal Challenge:

List at least five things (or more) you can do to help change your thinking and your attitude whenever you feel like you are losing hope.

- -

- -

- -

- -

- -

* * *

Chapter 2: Expectations

- - - - - - - - - - - - - - - - - - -

Psalm 5:1-3
O Lord, hear me as I pray; pay attention to my
groaning. Listen to my cry for help, my King and my
God, for I pray to no one but You. Listen to my voice
in the morning, Lord. Each morning I bring my
requests to You and wait expectantly.

- - - - - - - - - - - - - - - - - - -

I don't know about you, but when I am hoping for and expecting something good and it doesn't turn out that way, I don't always respond very well. I can get especially surly when a promise is broken. In a work situation, the employers' legal wording in an offer letter or an employer's manual makes certain that all workers understand there is no contractual guarantee for the job. They are promising nothing, yet losing a job still feels like a broken promise, doesn't it?

One of many sayings pinned onto the walls of many cubicles of mine is this: *Life is 10% what happens to you and 90% how you react to it.* I put it there to remind myself that I control my reactions, and often that is all I can control. That truth is on a card in my Hope Box along with these other verses and quotes I am sharing with you. (If you haven't done so already, feel free to get some cards and create your own box. Go ahead. I'll wait.)

- - - - - - - - - - - - - - - - - - -

Experience is not what happens to you; it's what you do with what happens to you.
~ Aldous Huxley[vii]

- - - - - - - - - - - - - - - - - - -

Some people say just lower your expectations and then it won't hurt so much, and then you will avoid disappointment. Really? If you never expect anything good, how can you hope for anything?

Is it really an impossible situation or is it an opportunity?

How is it faith if you expect nothing?

And it is not faith if you know what is going to happen next!

- - - - - - - - - - - - - - - - - - -

Psalm 91:2
This I declare about the Lord: He alone is my refuge,
my place of safety; He is my God, and I trust him.

- - - - - - - - - - - - - - - - - - -

Michelangelo warned that we don't aim too high and miss it, but instead that we aim too low and succeed.

Applying this truth to the job search, how high should we be aiming? The reality is not necessarily that we aim too high or too low. The number of months we have been out of work can sometimes change that aim, altering the amount of income we will accept or the position we will take. My expectations of the workplace have definitely changed with the realities of getting a job in this economy.

Companies interviewing have their own expectations and bias of what type of position or salary we will or should accept. Right?

The years of experience on my resume immediately create suspicion if I apply for an entry level position. Even though I am willing to do the work, to take the cut in pay, they don't believe it, or so they say, in one way or another. But their attitudes are not anything I can control.

* * *

I sat on the north side of the huge oval conference table, across from two recruiters and one account manager for an inside sales position, each of them asking me the same questions differently.

"Why would you want to sit on the phone making 100 outbound calls every day?"

I had answered the first recruiter, "because my track record shows that I would do it well, and exceed expectations and be able to move into a more diverse role within a couple of years." The recruiter had initially assured me the position had a growth path.

The account manager asked me the same question but she did not appear to believe my answer, or so her attitude and follow up questions indicated.

"Where else are you interviewing?" she asked.

It didn't occur to me quickly enough to ask why she was asking, or to tell her it was none of her business. So I answered honestly and told her about the office manager position I was waiting to hear back on, and she pounced on that.

"Oh you would be an excellent office manager, and it would use so many more of your skills." And with that she stood up and ended the meeting. The first recruiter caught my eye and shrugged her shoulders.

I just shook my head as I drove home wondering what had just happened, as I replayed the conversations in my mind, wondering if I had blown it or if once again, that's just not where God wants me. I choose to believe the latter.

Despite multiple follow up emails, I never heard back on the office manager position either.

So I keep searching for where God wants to place me, keep walking through every open door, and keep my attitude right when my expectations are not met and/or the door closes.

The time will come and I pray I will understand at that time. But even if I never fully understand, that's okay, because I know that he is the Almighty God, and he knows everything I am experiencing.

Perhaps it is not for me to understand.

- - - - - - - - - - - - - - - - - - -

Ecclesiastes 3:11 CEV
God makes everything happen at the right time. Yet
none of us can ever fully understand all that He has
done, and He puts questions in our minds about the
past and the future.

- - - - - - - - - - - - - - - - - - -

As I heard in a sermon, You can't choose your crosses, but you can choose your responses.

Regardless of my expectations, how I respond to this reality is my choice and is all part of the growth process on this journey.

- - - - - - - - - - - - - - - - - - -

James 1:2-4
Dear brothers and sisters, when troubles come your
way, consider it an opportunity for great joy. For you
know that when your faith is tested, your endurance
has a chance to grow. So let it grow, for when your
endurance is fully developed, you will be perfect and
complete, needing nothing.

- - - - - - - - - - - - - - - - - - -

Having faith that is being tested means that my endurance is growing. When God chooses to answer differently than I pray, I accept his answer as the right decision. No matter what.

That is so much easier to say than do, and I have occasional mini pity parties along the way, but I believe it is truth and I strive to practice it.

* * *

My Accidental Sabbatical includes daily encouragement and hope from the books by Os Hillman, *Today God Is First (TGIF) Volumes 1 and 2.*viii

His daily devotionals from these two books arrive via email and I have read them for several years now. Each year my circumstances may be different, or may not, but the truths he shares never change, in or out of the workplace.

Recently he wrote: God never said **when** he was going to deliver Moses. He just said he would. And Moses did not hesitate to question God about it!

– – – – – – – – – – – – – – – – – – – –

Exodus 5:23
Ever since I came to Pharaoh as Your spokesman, he has been even more brutal to Your people. And You have done nothing to rescue them!

– – – – – – – – – – – – – – – – – – – –

Many times in my life I have noticed that God's timetable and mine do not coincide. This Accidental Sabbatical is no exception. I may have technically chosen to leave my job when I joined my husband. But I did not choose to have my career on hold and be without income for this long, much less forever. I struggle with these issues, maybe not daily, but certainly more often than I would like.

With that struggle, I continually remind myself of the fact that He is God. I am not.

Some days I say it over and over again.

He is God. I am not.

- - - - - - - - - - - - - - - - - - -

Deuteronomy 7:9
Understand, therefore, that the Lord your God is indeed God. He is the faithful God who keeps His covenant for a thousand generations and lavishes His unfailing love on those who love Him and obey His commandments.

- - - - - - - - - - - - - - - - - - -

So it is all about my expectations and how I manage them. What am I expecting of myself? Of God? Of others? Of the workplace?

Could I alleviate any of the pain by expecting less, without settling for less? Or am I to accept that God knows best and patiently wait for it?

- - - - - - - - - - - - - - - - - - -

Psalm 130:5
I am counting on the Lord; yes, I am counting on him. I have put my hope in his word.

- - - - - - - - - - - - - - - - - - -

Your work is going to fill a large part of your life, and the only way to do great work is to love what you do. If you haven't found it yet, keep looking. Don't settle.
~ Steve Jobs[ix]

- - - - - - - - - - - - - - - - - - -

Structural unemployment is defined as a specific type of unemployment directly resulting from fundamental economic changes, longer lasting than a cyclical unemployment that could be improved by increasing demand. Yet if some of the economists can be believed, this structural unemployment simultaneously includes the possibility for new and different jobs opening up in other areas of the economy.

My personal Accidental Sabbatical is definitely a direct result of economic changes in our world. Is yours?

Even as I search for those new and different jobs in other areas of the economy I realize that no matter what type of unemployment this is that we are enduring, it is an obstacle to overcome.

Whenever I overcome an obstacle, I end up stronger.

What will those obstacles help me become this time?

* * *

Ageism is prejudice or discrimination on the basis of a person's age. There is no denying that reality. The president of a local recruiting firm gave a presentation at the weekly job seeker meeting, and she had these tips for job seekers over 40:

1. Use hair color. Especially women. Men are considered "distinguished" with gray hair; women, not so much.

2. If the clothes you have are more than 3 years old, buy 2 new suits or outfits that are in trend, and wear them to all networking functions and job interviews.

3. Exercise, drink lots of water, take care of your physical body so that you look and feel vivacious and energetic.

I then listened to her provide one reason after another why I would most likely never again be hired for a "regular" job. She explained that her intent was not to be depressing but to try to help us all understand the realities of the marketplace now.

As I drove home, I began to feel depressed; but I stopped myself and instead came away from that meeting determined to create my own opportunities. I became determined to find a way to offer my skills and services where they are needed and not to worry or be focused on a paycheck. As Seth Godin said in a recent webinar, *Don't keep track of the money. Keep track of the engagement. The money follows.*

* * *

We do have to understand perception and keep our expectations in line with reality if we are to survive and thrive.

As they say, perception is reality.

Until it is not.

I surrender my anxiety about obstacles to the Lord constantly, because I know that if I trust him, he will help me. Absolutely. It is not based on a feeling; it is a fact in my life.

Most of the obstacles to employment these days are not things that we can control.

We can change our hair color but not our age.

We can change our resumes to include only the last 10 or 15 years, but we cannot erase the experience. We have lived it.

We can decide that we will accept any position that utilizes at least some of our skills and provides for at least some of our financial needs.

But we cannot make them hire us just because we are willing.

- - - - - - - - - - - - - - - - - - -

Psalm 37:5
Commit everything you do to the LORD. Trust him,
and he will help you.

- - - - - - - - - - - - - - - - - - -

As Pastor Rick Warren recently posted on Facebook:
Just start doing what you know is the right thing to do and the feelings will follow. Don't wait. Action ignites motivation.[x]

* * *

I believe it is a blessing when things don't go as I plan or hope they will! Maybe not one that I can see right away, but definitely a blessing. So much so that I almost don't experience disappointment anymore. Almost. Okay, I'm not perfect. But I have seen those blessings more than once in my life, so now I can at least step back sooner to look at the bigger picture. Much sooner anyway.

Because I know that God will work it all together for my good.

- -

Romans 8:28
And we know that God causes everything to work together for the good of those who love God and are called according to His purpose for them.

- -

As the saying goes from that prolific writer, Unknown, Everything works out in the end. If it hasn't worked out, it's not the end.

* * *

When the Human Resources guy first called me to conduct a phone interview I was thrilled. Despite the fact that this tech company would be a 70-mile daily commute, I was hopeful that it would be a career job that would make it worthwhile. The phone interview went well, so next came the onsite interview set for the following week. I was ecstatic!

That next Wednesday I drove that nearly hour long commute in rush hour traffic. Then I spent a full day in what turned out to be a group interview – eight different managers with five different candidates sat in the conference room, rectangular tables forming a large square. We were interviewed all together taking turns answering questions and then individually. I have had more than one of these group interviews or 'panel interviews' now; and if you have as well, you know what I'm talking about.

Among my competition was a twenty-something new grad, fresh with her new shiny black pumps and very short black skirt and jacket, trying to land her first job. She smiled and bobbed her blonde curls around as she asked me questions while we were waiting for the interview to begin, questions that HR could not legally have asked me, such as if I had any kids and how old they were.

I wore my interview suit and my hair in a not-too-stuffy but professional bun at the nape of my neck. I felt old and very out of place.

Right about then a brunette walked in the lobby door and ran up and greeted the blonde with a hug. She said loudly how excited she was to see her there and assured her she had put in a good word for her.

Even though I thought the interviews had gone well, I knew as I drove home that I would not get an offer. I knew that I did not fit into their culture, and that even though *I* felt I could overcome that and succeed, culture fit is a mandatory requirement. Culture fit beats skillset any day.

When I called the next Monday to follow up with the HR guy who had originally done my phone interview, he asked when I was available to interview. He went on to tell me that interviews are held on Wednesdays.

He did not even remember me.

I reminded him that I had already been to the group interview the previous Wednesday. Long silence. Then the back pedaling response, "Oh. Well I'll get back to you on that", and of course I never heard another word from him.

Expectations. Hopes dashed. Again I fought off depression.

But I have seen that same job posting at the beginning of every quarter since then. And less than 30 days after that interview, the company announced another huge layoff and I knew then that I had been spared and that *not* getting hired was the blessing. Even so, that did not eliminate the disappointment I had felt.

- - - - - - - - - - - - - - - - - - -

2 Corinthians 4:18
So we don't look at the troubles we can see now;
rather, we fix our gaze on things that cannot be seen.
For the things we see now will soon be gone, but the
things we cannot see will last forever.

- - - - - - - - - - - - - - - - - - -

I trust the plan even when I don't see the path.

- - - - - - - - - - - - - - - - - - -

I encourage you to accept that you may not be able to
see a path right now, but that doesn't mean it's not
there.
~ Nick Vujicic[xi]

- - - - - - - - - - - - - - - - - - -

I remind myself again to trust the plan even when I don't see the path.

- -

Jeremiah 29:11
For I know the plans I have for you, declares the Lord,
plans to prosper you and not to harm you, plans to
give you hope and a future.

- - - - - - - - - - - - - - - - - - -

I intentionally focus on the positive, yet I don't discount the truth. We have to work within the reality of the job market as it is today. We have to admit what we can and cannot change and do what we can do.

* * *

Personal Challenge:

What expectations do you have, of yourself, and of the job market?

How do those expectations coincide with the reality that you have experienced in your Accidental Sabbatical?

- -

- - - - - - - - - - - - - - - - - - - -

- -

- - - - - - - - - - - - - - - - - - - -

- - - - - - - - - - - - - - - - - - - -

- - - - - - - - - - - - - - - - - - - -

- - - - - - - - - - - - - - - - - - - -

- -

- -

What can you personally change to help bring your expectations in line with reality?

- -

- -

- -

- -

- -

- -

- -

* * *

Chapter 3: Waiting

- - - - - - - - - - - - - - - - - -

Psalm 27:14
Wait patiently for the Lord; Be brave and courageous.
Yes, wait patiently for the Lord.

- - - - - - - - - - - - - - - - - -

Waiting feels like hope on hold.

Occasionally it occurs to me that God has not changed my circumstances yet, and that he may not even be planning to! Perhaps that is because he is working on changing *me* instead. C.S. Lewis said that he didn't pray to change God's mind, but to change his own mind. I know when I pray that it changes my frame of mind.

Prayer for me, during a long waiting period like this one, vacillates between earnest pleas for help, and angrily asking God if He is listening at all, then asking forgiveness for forgetting to whom I am talking. (I periodically read Job 38 when I need a reminder!)

- - - - - - - - - - - - - - - - - - -

Psalm 50:15
Then call on me when you are in trouble, and I will
rescue you, and you will give me glory.

- - - - - - - - - - - - - - - - - - -

I remind God when I pray that we still have an unsold house in another state. And then in the next breath, I remind myself that the house is his house, not ours. We are simply stewards of his resources. I am not to worry about it. I am not to worry about anything for that matter. The future is his to take care of, not mine.

As Pete Wilson preached, When we worry, we are assuming a position in the universe that we don't own!

So while I thank God for meeting all of my needs I also ask him to take away my worry. I *need* to not worry and he will meet that need. I need to just give it up to him daily. Multiple times in a day if necessary, and many days it is necessary.

I know that my prayers are changing me, because my prayers have changed.

- - - - - - - - - - - - - - - - - - -

Philippians 4:6
Don't worry about anything; instead, pray about
everything. Tell God what you need, and thank Him
for all He has done.

- - - - - - - - - - - - - - - - - - -

I am not worrying. I am praying. I praise God for everything he has done. I know in my heart that just because I see nothing happening right now, doesn't mean it isn't happening or won't happen in the future.

- - - - - - - - - - - - - - - - -

Do not trouble your hearts overmuch with thought of the road tonight. Maybe the paths that you shall each tread are already laid before your feet, though you do not see them. ~ Tolkien[xii]

- - - - - - - - - - - - - - - - -

I am waiting and praying and watching for the path.

Don't worry. Pray.

God knows what we need, so we ask him and we thank him.

What if what I really need is not what I am praying for?

What if the entire purpose of the wait is to teach me how to pray and how not to worry?

What if this journey has nothing to do with a job, but everything to do with God knowing what I need instead?

* * *

We have a bird feeder in our front yard, and I often sit and watch the chickadees and cardinals take turns getting their fill. I think about this verse as I watch them eat and fly away, come back for more, and eat and fly away. They don't pile up the seeds like the squirrels amass their acorns. They just eat and fly.

- - - - - - - - - - - - - - - - - - -

Matthew 6:25-28

That is why I tell you not to worry about everyday life — whether you have enough food and drink, or enough clothes to wear. Isn't life more than food, and your body more than clothing? Look at the birds. They don't plant or harvest or store food in barns, for your heavenly Father feeds them. And aren't you far more valuable to him than they are? Can all your worries add a single moment to your life?

And why worry about your clothing? Look at the lilies of the field and how they grow. They don't work or make their clothing, yet Solomon in all his glory was not dressed as beautifully as they are. And if God cares so wonderfully for wildflowers that are here today and thrown into the fire tomorrow, He will certainly care for you. Why do you have so little faith?

- - - - - - - - - - - - - - - - - -

If I keep my focus on the Lord and don't stress, it is all good. The truth is, I have to choose where I'm going to focus.

- - - - - - - - - - - - - - - - - -

Corrie Ten Boom wrote:
If you look at the world, you'll be distressed.
If you look within, you'll be depressed.
But if you look at Christ, you'll be at rest.

- - - - - - - - - - - - - - - - - -

When I was a teenager, Corrie Ten Boom spoke at our church and because my father was the pastor of the church, we were honored to be able to take her out for dinner. She is authentic. If you have not read any of her books, you would be blessed by them, especially *The Hiding Place*. Her message is one of forgiveness, hope and love in action, having lived through the holocaust and escaping, after witnessing her family's executions.

- - - - - - - - - - - - - - - - - - - -

2 Thessalonians 3:16
Now may the Lord of peace Himself give you His peace at all times and in every situation.

- - - - - - - - - - - - - - - - - - - -

I have always been a voracious reader, but especially during this Accidental Sabbatical, I am reading books that will help me grow personally and professionally, as well as stories that will strengthen my faith and give me hope and peace. One of the huge blessings for me right now, is that I have this time to read, without guilt, while I wait.

What books have been life-changing for you?

Here is a list of some of the books I have been reading; some business, some personal growth and other classics I read years ago and have been re-reading. Some of these I haven't yet finished reading, but I will and I believe they are all worthy of your time as well.

Shari Risoff

Here is a list of books that have blessed me, taught me, and entertained me. I recommend them. (in alpha order by title except the first):

– – – – – – – – – – – – – – – – – – –

* *The Bible (Message or NLT version -my preference)*
* *7 Habits of Highly Effective People, by Stephen R. Covey*
* *A Place of Healing, by Joni Earekson Tada*
* *Bird by Bird, by Anne Lamott*
* *Body of Work, by Pamela Slim*
* *Change Agent, by Os Hillman*
* *Choose Joy, by Kay Warren*
* *Daring Greatly, by Brené Brown*
* *Escape From Cubicle Nation, by Pamela Slim*
* *The Happiness Advantage: The Seven Principles of Positive Psychology that Fuel Success and Performance at Work, by Shawn Achor*
* *Neanderthals at Work: How People and Politics Can Drive You Crazy... And What You Can Do About Them, by Albert J. Bernstein and Sydney Craft Rozen*
* *Plan B, by Pete Wilson*
* *Principle-Centered Leadership, by Stephen R. Covey*
* *Purpose Driven Life, by Rick Warren*
* *Social Media Explained, by Mark Schaeffer*
* *Strengthfinders 2.0, by Tom Rath*
* *Tribes, by Seth Godin*
* *Upside of Irrationality, by Dan Ariely*

What to Say When you Talk to Yourself, by Shad Helmstetter
And also some great fiction …
* *1984, by George Orwell*
* *Atlas Shrugged, by Ayn Rand*
* *Brave New World, by Aldous Huxley*
* *Chronicles of the Nephilim series, by Brian Godawa*
* *Spillworthy, by Johanna Harness*

- -

These books come from diverse people and mindsets and are just some of the books that have entertained, educated and helped me learn more about myself and my strengths and how those fit into and affect my career.

Reading memoirs and fiction takes me into another world, another time and place, allowing me to escape from the realities of my Accidental Sabbatical if even for a few hours, allowing me to see the world through someone else's eyes.

If you have already read these books or want other recommendations, go to Quora.com and type in the question: "What are some potentially life-changing books?" You will find many more to add to the list.

One of the biggest challenges is learning to just be.

Be alone.

Be content.

For many of us, it is easier to *do* than to *be*.

Reading helps me to be still while I sit and wait.

- -

Psalm 40:1-3

I waited patiently for the LORD to help me, and He turned to me and heard my cry. He lifted me out of the pit of despair, out of the mud and the mire. He set my feet on solid ground and steadied me as I walked along. He has given me a new song to sing, a hymn of praise to our God. Many will see what He has done and be amazed. They will put their trust in the LORD.

- -

Some days I wait patiently, other days not so much.

I look forward to the day when I will be rejoicing and praising because my prayers for work have been answered. Nowhere in the Bible does it say that God solves our problems with the solutions we give him. Like this Psalm says, David waited patiently and the Lord heard his cry. Then when God did move, it was because of what God had done, that many saw it and were amazed and put their trust in Him.

I want to be just that patient, and to see God move in my life in such a way that it will amaze and encourage me and others. It's not hard to see how the following quote ended up in my Hope Box, is it? This particular bit of wisdom is helpful to me when I'm not feeling so patient:

- -

Do not be impatient with your seemingly slow progress. Do not try to run faster than you presently can. If you are studying, reflecting and trying, you are making progress whether you are aware of it or not. A traveler walking the road in the darkness of night is still going forward. Someday, some way, everything will break open, like the natural unfolding of a rosebud.

~ Vernon Howard[xiii]

- - - - - - - - - - - - - - - - - - -

Romans 12:12
Rejoice in our confident hope. Be patient in trouble, and keep on praying.

- - - - - - - - - - - - - - - - - - -

God does hear and he does provide. How he chooses to do so has amazed me in the past, and then his answers to prayer become remembered miracles. The Israelites piled up stones to remind them to share the miracles with their children. Even though I have not physically piled up stones, I have experiences, blessings and memories that I visualize that way. I pray for his help and then I wait. I wait for him to answer and I know his answer will be far better than what I could come up with on my own.

- - - - - - - - - - - - - - - - - - -

2 Corinthians 9:8
And God will generously provide all you need. Then you will always have everything you need and plenty left over to share with others.

- - - - - - - - - - - - - - - - - - -

I am not going to lie. I am always disappointed when I am rejected, especially when I really wanted the job. One day when I was feeling particularly low a friend sent me a note that was a gift of hope from God through him. It said, God always answers prayer. Sometimes the answer is 'yes'. Sometimes 'not yet'. And other times, 'I've got something better in mind.'

I can imagine God smiling when he says that.

There are times I have thanked God for *not* choosing to use the solutions I suggested to him in my prayers, because he always had something better in mind.

– – – – – – – – – – – – – – – – – – –

I recommend you take care of the minutes and the hours will take care of themselves.
~ Earl of Chesterfield[xiv]

– – – – – – – – – – – – – – – – – – –

Personal Challenge:

How are you waiting? What are you doing with your minutes every day? What will you do today to help someone else while they wait?

– – – – – – – – – – – – – – – – – – – –

– – – – – – – – – – – – – – – – – – – –

– – – – – – – – – – – – – – – – – – – –

– – – – – – – – – – – – – – – – – – – –

* * *

Chapter 4: Change

Where do we find hope when change seems to be the only constant?

This Accidental Sabbatical is changing me in many ways. Every day. I am sure it is changing you too. It definitely changes your daily schedule, the environment where you will spend your time. And it will change you on the inside too... whether or not it is good change or bad change, is up to you. It really is your choice.

We know that positive change requires getting out of ruts and comfort zone and feeling out of place when it is new.

I am trying to make this change process positive in my life. I cannot always change my circumstances, but I can change how I think about them and control how I react to them. I can choose joy and hope and know that I am in God's hands.

I remind myself. It is my choice.

Every day I get to choose.

– – – – – – – – – – – – – – – – – – –

1 Thessalonians 5:16-18
Always be joyful.
Never stop praying.
Be thankful in all circumstances, for this is God's will
for you who belong to Christ Jesus.

- - - - - - - - - - - - - - - - - - - -

How do you respond when you are faced with change that you did not create and do not want?

- - - - - - - - - - - - - - - - - - - -

Everyone has gone through something that has
changed them in a way that they could never go back
to the person they once were. ~ Unknown

- - - - - - - - - - - - - - - - - - - -

Jillian Michaels smiles at me from her workout video as she says *Get comfortable with being uncomfortable.* It's as if she is right here with me in the living room seeing my discomfort.

She says this because she knows that discomfort is a necessary step in the process.

- - - - - - - - - - - - - - - - - - - -

One can choose to go back toward safety or forward
toward growth. Growth must be chosen again and
again; fear must be overcome again and again.
~ Abraham Maslow[xv]

- - - - - - - - - - - - - - - - - - - -

A few years ago my manager informed me that we were going to be relocating from one building to another. Our current building was farthest away from the main campus of buildings, and we had more freedom than others. We had no security guard at the front desk, and not even a badge reader to swipe in and out. We used old fashioned keys to get in the door.

After three years I had finally negotiated a corner cubicle with a window and he knew I was attached to it.

He knew this would not be change I would choose.

Not. Ever.

They were sending us into work spaces not even large enough to be called individual cubes, and the badge reader in that building failed to work at least 50% of the time, leaving us stranded at the door in snow or rain or whatever the weather. It felt like a demotion and like a huge slap in the face for years of good work. During my career, in several different jobs, I have relocated multiple times and this was the first time that the resources were being downgraded. Relocation usually meant a new and bigger building, or at least a better environment. Not this time.

I did not handle the change too well at first. But I came to the realization that I had a choice. I could either find a new job or I could deal with it. Period. I chose to stay until the situation could otherwise be changed.

It has now changed. I never have to see that mini cube again!

We always have a choice of some sort.

This Accidental Sabbatical may not have been a choice, however we still have a choice in how we adapt.

— — — — — — — — — — — — — — — — — — — —

Adapt or perish, now as ever, is nature's inexorable imperative.
~ *H.G. Wells*[xvi]

— — — — — — — — — — — — — — — — — — —

So I adapt!

Here is my ever-growing list of things to do for positive change during this Accidental Sabbatical …

1. Learn something new! Enroll in an online Massive Open Online Course (MOOC), free on multiple sites such as Coursera.org.

2. Take a yoga class. Try out a free class in a studio. Or just do yoga at home with the Bryan Kest CD or watching it on YouTube. (Note: see the Resources chapter for links to these ideas.)

3. Volunteer somewhere. Deliver meals to the homeless or help build houses with Habitat for Humanity. Or search volunteermatch.org and find something in your area that interests you and matches your skill set.

4. Help people in their job search. Create resumes and cover letters or role-play for interviews and share job postings that might interest them.

5. Attend networking events such as a LinkedIn Live event in your town, or a job seeker group, or other

groups with people who share your interests. You can find any number of networking possibilities at meetup.com. You never know whom you will meet and how you can help someone else on this journey. Or you may in turn meet someone who will help with your search.

6. Cardio Workout. This one is my greatest personal challenge. I know physical exercise is good for the brain, the body, and psyche. I still don't have this habit mastered, but I keep working on it.

7. Be at peace alone. Give your mind a chance to just think, or not think.

8. Find someone to help! Someone out there needs help and you have the help they need.

* * *

One unemployed accountant spent an afternoon at his church helping the bookkeeper with QuickBooks and explaining what the CPA would need from her at yearend.

Some non-profit organizations welcome and appreciate anyone willing to volunteer to fold letters, stuff and stamp envelopes in a mailing campaign. Sometimes they will even provide lunch in appreciation.

Meetup.com can help you find a group or start a group with similar interests and skills.

Do what you can to help others and to help yourself.

God will take care of the job. In his time.

— — — — — — — — — — — — — — — — — —

*We must be willing to let go of the life we planned so
as to have the life that is waiting for us.*
~ *Joseph Campbell*[xvii]

- - - - - - - - - - - - - - - - - - - -

What plan are you holding on to? I had a five-year plan and a ten-year plan. But three years in, something happened to change the trajectory of the plan. So do I hold on to the hope that somehow I can redirect it and get it back on the original course? Or do I let it go and move toward the new life ahead and a new plan? I personally have tried both ways.

In the beginning it seemed that perseverance could overcome, that just hanging in there was the solution. Sometimes that is the case. Other times, however, it does not work that way and we adjust our thinking and our plan. Does this mean that I should not make any plans? I think I will just write them in pencil and learn to erase.

In his book, *The 21 Irrefutable Laws of Leadership*, John Maxwell introduces his acrostic for the term PLAN AHEAD.

P: Predetermine a course of action

L: Lay out your goals

A: Adjust your priorities

N: Notify key personnel

A: Allow time for acceptance

H: Head into action

E: Expect problems

A: Always point to your successes

D: Daily review your progress

As J.P. Morgan said: The first step towards getting somewhere is to decide that you are not going to stay where you are.

Move out of your comfort zone! If you just relax, doing only what makes you comfortable, you will not grow. This challenge is very difficult for me. It is much easier to just stay comfortable right there in that rut.

I was apprehensive about doing a live interview on a blogtalk radio show to share with people about my book. But I did it! It was a tremendously satisfying experience because I confronted my fear. On top of that, I learned that I could speak in public and survive.

Now I have yet another date on the calendar to speak at a book club meeting. Am I nervous? You bet. But I will face that fear again and it will stretch me when I do.

What are you hoping will change in your life?

What are you courageously changing today?

If we continue walking in our ruts and don't push out of a comfort zone, how will we ever find a new path?

* * *

— — — — — — — — — — — — — — — — — — —

Take care of your body. It's the only place you have to live. ~ Jim Rohn[xviii]

— — — — — — — — — — — — — — — — — — —

I have changed in many ways during these long months on this journey. I believe that most, if not all of the changes have been positive ones. A lifestyle change toward a healthy living goal has been to have a green smoothie for breakfast every morning. It has been consistent for more than a year now.

This green drink consists of the fruits and vegetables that I need for the entire day, and provides clarity of thought that I did not know was missing. A friend who must eat gluten-free and dairy-free, sent me to the incrediblesmoothies.com website where there are several recipe options, many of which I tried before coming up with one combination that my husband also enjoys with me.

Here is my basic green smoothie recipe (2 servings):

* 1 banana

* 1 apple

* ½ cup pineapple

* ½ cup unsweetened almond milk (or unsweetened almond/coconut milk)

* 2 cups kale

* 3 cups spinach

* Ice cubes

Blend until smooth.

Add ice water to thin, or more ice cubes to thicken.

I often add a few grapes to sweeten it, or sometimes an orange for a sharp citrus tang. You can also add flaxseed or chia seeds for fiber and protein.

I was surprised to find that it actually tastes good and now I am hooked! (Other smoothie recipes can be found at the link in the Resources section).

Another change I am making this year is to be boldly transparent with what I share. I am careful not to over-share details of life, especially in social media. For example, you will never see me post a photo of an amazing dinner that I've prepared. This chosen transparency I'm talking about is a decision to be real in front of others. Real. Flawed. Frightened of change. Breathing deeply as I walk out of the comfort zone and into the unknown.

- - - - - - - - - - - - - - - - - -

You will never change your life until you change something you do daily.
~ Mike Murdoch[xix]

- - - - - - - - - - - - - - - - - -

Personal Challenge:

Describe what "good change" means to you.

What big goals do you have for your own personal change?

What will you do today to help yourself navigate change to meet those goals?

- - - - - - - - - - - - - - - - - - -
- - - - - - - - - - - - - - - - - - -
- - - - - - - - - - - - - - - - - - -
- - - - - - - - - - - - - - - - - - -
- - - - - - - - - - - - - - - - - - -

* * *

Chapter 5: Security

— — — — — — — — — — — — — — — — —

Philippians 4:12-13
I know how to live on almost nothing or with
everything. I have learned the secret of living in every
situation, whether it is with a full stomach or empty,
with plenty or little. For I can do everything through
Christ who gives me strength.

— — — — — — — — — — — — — — — — —

Does hope make us feel secure?

The feeling of security can be financial or it can be found in a sense of belonging. It is tempting to look at a 401K or bank statement and think it provides security. It is easier to have faith for the future when you have six months or even years of expenses saved. But where does that sense of security come from when you are paying the mortgage or rent, and the ever-spiraling cost of health insurance, out of that dwindling 401K?

In my experience, security in money and material things is only a fallacy. And we all know that 'job security' no longer exists. Wouldn't you agree?

Joni Eareckson Tada wrote in one of her daily devotionals: People are only as secure as the source of their security. Christian psychologists say that good mental health springs from two things: security and significance. Security in who we are and significance in what we do. Since Christ is the source of peace, joy, strength, and rest, and in him we live and move and have our very being, we can be secure and feel significant when we place our trust in Jesus.

What happens when the money is gone? If it has been your source of hope, you will have no peace.

I know what it means to be broke and to be hungry, to gather pennies and search for loose change on the car floor or under a couch cushion to buy a can of soup or a gallon of gas. Been there. It is not fun, but it is not the end of the world either.

It builds character. So does hope.

God is my source of that hope.

- - - - - - - - - - - - - - - - - - - -

Romans 15:13
I pray that God, the source of hope, will fill you completely with joy and peace because you trust in Him. Then you will overflow with confident hope through the power of the Holy Spirit.

- - - - - - - - - - - - - - - - - - - -

I feel more intelligent when I hang out with intelligent people, don't you? And I believe I am actually smarter because of interacting with them. Conversely I can get equally negative when I listen to negativity and allow those toxins into my life.

I become like the people with whom I spend time.

We all do.

When I was growing up, we moved every couple of years. The need to find my place or a way to fit in was a huge factor in my life, and was always difficult. Many times I made bad choices.

Jim Rohn said that we become the combined average of the five people we hang around the most. Think about your five people. Are you spending your time with positive influences? Visualize the person you become when you are made up of the combined average of those five people. Is that who you really are?

More importantly, is that who you want to be?

Warren Buffet said It's better to hang out with people better than you. Pick out associates whose behavior is better than yours, and you'll drift in that direction.

- - - - - - - - - - - - - - - - - - - -

Psalm 32:8
The Lord says, I will guide you along the best pathway for your life. I will advise you and watch over you.

- - - - - - - - - - - - - - - - - - - -

This move across country that resulted in my Accidental Sabbatical has put me on a new path once again. I pray for good things to happen in my life. It may be scary at times, but whenever I let negativity in, I meet someone who has it tougher than I do and I am reminded that God is the source of my confidence.

- - - - - - - - - - - - - - - - - - - -

Jeremiah 17:7
But blessed are those who trust in the Lord and have made the Lord their hope and confidence.

- - - - - - - - - - - - - - - - - - - -

Security is defined as the state of being free from fear, danger or threat. Freedom from doubt or anxiety. It occurs to me that feeling secure is also a choice; making the decision to not let fear rule.

- - - - - - - - - - - - - - - - - - - -

Isaiah 40:31
Those who trust in the Lord will find new strength. They will soar high on wings like eagles. They will run and not grow weary. They will walk and not faint.

- - - - - - - - - - - - - - - - - - - -

Without fear I am able to trust.
What I do today directly impacts my tomorrow.
Anne Lamott explains it perfectly...

- - - - - - - - - - - - - - - - - - - -

I have a lot of faith. But I am also afraid a lot, and have no real certainty about anything. I remembered something Father Tom had told me – that the opposite of faith is not doubt, but certainty. Certainty is missing the point entirely. Faith includes noticing the mess, the emptiness and discomfort, and letting it be there until some light returns.
~ Anne Lamott[xx]

- - - - - - - - - - - - - - - - - - - -

Some days when I read the Psalms, I just want to crawl into the cave and repeat the words out loud after him.

- - - - - - - - - - - - - - - - - - - -

Psalm 69:1-3
Save me, O God, for the floodwaters are up to my neck. Deeper and deeper I sink into the mire; I can't find a foothold. I am in deep water, and the floods overwhelm me. I am exhausted from crying for help; my throat is parched. My eyes are swollen with weeping, waiting for my God to help me.

- - - - - - - - - - - - - - - - - - - -

I echo what he wrote in so many of the psalms and feel the same deep emotions that he did. I share their anger when I hear stories from people who lost their jobs due to injustice and discrimination, because of age, race, gender, or any of the other 'protected groups'. It isn't fair and we don't see any justice. But life has never been fair.

However, I believe in the law of cause and effect. I know it to be true because I have seen it happen more than once.

I have to leave it in God's hands.

- - - - - - - - - - - - - - - - - - - -

Psalm 37:3-5
Trust in the Lord and do good. Then you will live safely in the land and prosper. Take delight in the Lord, and He will give you your heart's desires. Commit everything you do to the Lord. Trust Him, and He will help you.

- - - - - - - - - - - - - - - - - - - -

I trust. I am holding on to this verse and my hope is in the Lord. I am not afraid and I am calm.

- - - - - - - - - - - - - - - - - - - -

Exodus 14:13
Don't be afraid. Just stand still and watch the Lord rescue you today... The Lord himself will fight for you. Just stay calm.

- - - - - - - - - - - - - - - - - - - -

And while some might say I'm just a "believer", in the *Neanderthals at Work*[xxi] definition, (and they would be right), I believe that God is fighting for us and will vindicate those who have been wronged. One day it will all catch up with them. Some call it karma but whatever you want to call it, I know from my own life that it happens.

What goes around in life definitely comes around.

Have you been caught in a trap?

– – – – – – – – – – – – – – – – – – –

Genesis 50:20
You intended to harm me, but God intended it all for good.

– – – – – – – – – – – – – – – – – – –

Nothing that has ever happened to you has escaped God's notice. You can trust that He will bring to account everyone who has hurt you, in His time and in His way. ~ Kay Arthur[xxii]

– – – – – – – – – – – – – – – – – – –

Yes! God has seen everything. He will make it right. In time. I believe it.

As I read the first 28 verses in the 35th chapter of the Psalms, I think specifically of people who were terminated without cause or who were set up to fail, and for others in this community who are sick with despair at this point. There are people unable to support themselves or their families, who are living on savings or credit cards. For many people the bank account is empty and their emotional bank account of hope is empty as well.

Anyone who has been set up to fail in the battle of corporate politics will resonate with David's prayer.

It's a long passage, but definitely worth the time to meditate on it.

– – – – – – – – – – – – – – – – – –

Psalm 35:1-28

A psalm of David.

O LORD, oppose those who oppose me. Fight those who fight against me. Put on your armor, and take up your shield. Prepare for battle, and come to my aid. Lift up Your spear and javelin against those who pursue me. Let me hear You say, "I will give you victory!" Bring shame and disgrace on those trying to kill me; turn them back and humiliate those who want to harm me. Blow them away like chaff in the wind – a wind sent by the angel of the LORD. Make their path dark and slippery, with the angel of the LORD pursuing them. I did them no wrong, but they laid a trap for me. I did them no wrong, but they dug a pit to catch me. So let sudden ruin come upon them! Let them be caught in the trap they set for me! Let them be destroyed in the pit they dug for me.

Then I will rejoice in the LORD. I will be glad because He rescues me. With every bone in my body I will praise him: "LORD, who can compare with You? Who else rescues the helpless from the strong? Who else protects the helpless and poor from those who rob them?"

Malicious witnesses testify against me. They accuse me of crimes I know nothing about. They repay me evil for good. I am sick with despair. Yet when they were ill, I grieved for them. I denied myself by fasting for them, but my prayers returned unanswered. I was sad, as though they were my friends or family, as if I were grieving for my own mother. But they are glad now that I am in trouble; they gleefully join together against me. I am attacked by people I don't even know; they slander me constantly. They mock me and call me names; they snarl at me.

How long, O Lord, will You look on and do nothing? Rescue me from their fierce attacks. Protect my life from these lions! Then I will thank You in front of the great assembly. I will praise You before all the people. Don't let my treacherous enemies rejoice over my defeat. Don't let those who hate me without cause gloat over my sorrow. They don't talk of peace; they plot against innocent people who mind their own business. They shout, "Aha! Aha! With our own eyes we saw him do it!"

O LORD, You know all about this. Do not stay silent. Do not abandon me now, O Lord. Wake up! Rise to my defense! Take up my case, my God and my Lord.

Declare me not guilty, O LORD my God, for You give justice. Don't let my enemies laugh about me in my troubles. Don't let them say, "Look, we got what we wanted! Now we will eat him alive!"

May those who rejoice at my troubles be humiliated and disgraced. May those who triumph over me be covered with shame and dishonor. But give great joy to those who came to my defense. Let them continually say, "Great is the LORD, who delights in blessing his servant with peace!" Then I will proclaim Your justice, and I will praise You all day long.

– – – – – – – – – – – – – – – – – – – –

Some people have told me they were actually relieved when they lost their job for any number of reasons, and they believe that now they will find something better. Especially now when so many terminations are due to corporate politics, corporate downsizing or 'rightsizing'. I don't know the exact figure, but I would bet that by now millions of people fall into those categories.

How many people have been set up to fail?

How many have been falsely accused?

And because job security has been obliterated, where will we now find our security and sense of belonging?

Where do we put our hope?

– – – – – – – – – – – – – – – – – – – –

Isaiah 54:17 (NET)
No weapon forged to be used against you will succeed; you will refute everyone who tries to accuse you. This is what the Lord will do for His servants –
I will vindicate them, says the Lord.

– – – – – – – – – – – – – – – – – – – –

It would be great if God would always protect us instantly from any wrongful accusation and vindicate us on the spot, and maybe it does happen that way sometimes, just not in my experience.

God will definitely vindicate, he has promised that.

The truth will always win in the end.

It may not happen instantly but it *will* happen.

– –

Psalm 69:32
The humble will see their God at work and be glad.
Let all who seek God's help be encouraged.

– –

Many wise people have observed that security is a fallacy.

These cards are in my Hope Box, along with many more on this subject. I especially love this first one:

– –

If you want total security, go to prison. There you're
fed, clothed, given medical care and so on. The only
thing lacking… is freedom.
~ Dwight D. Eisenhower[xxiii]

– –

Security is mostly a superstition. It does not exist in
nature, nor do the children of men as a whole
experience it. Avoiding danger is no safer in the long
run than outright exposure. Life is either a daring
adventure, or nothing. ~ Helen Keller[xxiv]

- - - - - - - - - - - - - - - - - - -

The biggest mistake that you can make is to believe that you are working for somebody else. Job security is gone. The driving force of a career must come from the individual. Remember: Jobs are owned by the company, you own your career!
~ Earl Nightingale[xxv]

- - - - - - - - - - - - - - - - - - -

Nothing can bring a real sense of security into the home except true love. ~ Billy Graham[xxvi]

- - - - - - - - - - - - - - - - - - -

God is true love. I have only found true security in him.

- - - - - - - - - - - - - - - - - - -

Growth demands a temporary surrender of security. It may mean giving up familiar but limiting patterns, safe but unrewarding work, values no longer believed in, and relationships that have lost their meaning.
~ John C. Maxwell[xxvii]

- - - - - - - - - - - - - - - - - - -

* * *

Personal Challenge:

What makes you feel secure?

What, if any, of those things have been removed from your life and what replaces them?

- - - - - - - - - - - - - - - - - - -

_ _

_ _

_ _

What will you do today to help someone else feel secure with a sense of belonging?

_ _

_ _

_ _

_ _

_ _

* * *

Chapter 6: Surrender

- - - - - - - - - - - - - - - - - - - -

Here's what's surprising about making sense of your life in God's story: the story is not about you – it's about Him. He is both the author and the main character, and He has written you into His story to say something about Him!
~ Mike Wilkerson[xxviii]

- - - - - - - - - - - - - - - - - - - -

Hope is the ultimate surrender.

As I ponder every day what I am supposed to do next, and where God is going to place me, I remind myself of this truth. It is not about me. It is not *my* story. It is about what God gives me to do in his story, what part he gives me to play. I am thankful he has written me into the script.

I don't always wait patiently to see how it is going to turn out. However if a person gets better with practice, I am getting close to mastering patience.

- - - - - - - - - - - - - - - - - - - -

2 Chronicles 15:7
But as for you, be strong and courageous, for your
work will be rewarded.

- -

Have you ever noticed how hard a caterpillar has to work to become a butterfly?

- -

What the caterpillar calls the end of the world, the
Master calls a butterfly.
~ Richard Bach[xxix]

- -

Amazing strength comes out of overcoming a challenge so impossible that there is no way to survive and certainly no way to accomplish it on my own. When faced with an obstacle, I ask God to do it through me.

- -

Anytime God leads you to do something that has
God-size dimensions, you will face a crisis of belief.
When you face a crisis of belief, what you do next
reveals what you really believe about God.
~ Dr. Henry Blackaby[xxx]

- -

What do you do with a crisis of belief? Do you ultimately calm down and just give it over to God? Or does it take your confidence away? Does it depend on the situation that day?

_ _ _ _ _ _ _ _ _ _ _ _ _ _ _ _ _ _

Hebrews 11:1
Faith is the confidence that what we hope for will
actually happen; it gives us assurance about things
we cannot see.

_ _ _ _ _ _ _ _ _ _ _ _ _ _ _ _ _ _

I am learning that I can be confident that everything happening within and around me is all part of the plan and that if God has put it in front of me, there is a reason. He will get me through it. Even when I do not understand or see the big picture, I have peace.

_ _ _ _ _ _ _ _ _ _ _ _ _ _ _ _ _ _

John 16:33
I have told you all this so that you may have peace in
me. Here on earth you will have many trials and
sorrow. But take heart, because I have overcome the
world.

_ _ _ _ _ _ _ _ _ _ _ _ _ _ _ _ _ _

This Accidental Sabbatical is a process of becoming comfortable being alone with myself and waiting for my next assignment. Some of the steps in that process are very emotional. And I understand it from an intellectual level even as I experience it from an emotional level.

I am surrendering to the pruning so that I can look forward to far better things. I may not enjoy the pain, but I envision the new growth and the season of preparation that this sabbatical has given me. I am going to embrace it fully. I am not going to beat up on myself. Instead I am going to focus on what I am learning instead of what I have given up.

Don't get me wrong – none of this is easy. It is a daily conscious decision, and some days are better than others.

– –

Psalm 37:7
Be still in the presence of the Lord, and wait patiently for Him to act. Don't worry about evil people who prosper or fret about their wicked schemes.

– –

Rumi says it well:
Sorrow prepares you for joy. It violently sweeps everything out of your house, so that new joy can find space to enter. It shakes the yellow leaves from the bough of your heart, so that fresh green leaves can grow in their place. It pulls the rotten roots, so that new roots hidden beneath have room to grow. Whatever sorrow shakes from your heart, far better things will take their place. ~ Rumi[xxxi]

– –

Matthew 11:28
Then Jesus said, "Come to me, all of you who are weary and carry heavy burdens, and I will give you rest."

– –

There is more than one way to look at pain in life.

We have the option of giving the pain over to God and letting Him provide relief and rest from it. For many of us, this Accidental Sabbatical has become about resting our physical and mental selves, perhaps for the first time in many years.

Often we must give ourselves permission to rest.

- - - - - - - - - - - - - - - - - -

Rest is not idleness, and to lie sometimes on the grass under trees on a summer's day, listening to the murmur of the water, or watching the clouds float across the sky, is by no means a waste of time.
~ John Lubbock[xxxii]

- - - - - - - - - - - - - - - - - -

Why do we worry and think it is all up to us?

Doesn't it benefit us if sometime in life we are shaken up and pushed out of our comfort zone?

What does it take before we have hope in something more than ourselves?

- - - - - - - - - - - - - - - - - -

Psalm 8:3-4
When I look at the night sky and see the work of Your fingers – the moon and the stars You set in place – what are mere mortals that You should think about them, human beings that You should care for them?

- - - - - - - - - - - - - - - - - -

If this Accidental Sabbatical provides the impetus for us to surrender to becoming bolder, to going where we have never gone, to dreaming more, isn't that a good thing? Even on the days that it doesn't really feel that way, I know that this journey is building my faith.

- - - - - - - - - - - - - - - - - - -

Proverbs 3:5-6
Trust in the Lord with all your heart; do not depend on your own understanding. Seek His will in all you do and He will show you which path to take.

- - - - - - - - - - - - - - - - - - -

I have to just walk and trust, walk and trust, and keep on going.

- - - - - - - - - - - - - - - - - - -

The best way out is always through. ~ Robert Frost

- - - - - - - - - - - - - - - - - - -

Today I received an email response to a position I applied for several days ago. There is a person's name at the bottom of the email but the message sounds computer-generated to me. I am sure you have seen something like it:

Thank you for your interest in our Customer Service Manager position. We appreciate the time you have taken to present your qualifications to us. We will contact you if there is an interest in discussing employment opportunities. Additionally, we will keep your information on file and it may be evaluated with respect to other positions that become available in the future. We invite you to visit our website periodically to review new positions as they become available, and update your profile as needed. Please accept our best wishes for your continued success.

Doesn't that sound encouraging? Hmm. Not so much. At the beginning of this journey I would have been depressed for hours after receiving an impersonal turn down email like this. Now I am either realistic or just numb. Or both. But I accept it and move on.

Because here is what I know for sure: If that is not where the Lord wants to place me, I absolutely don't want to be there.

- - - - - - - - - - - - - - - - - - - -

Ecclesiastes 7:13-14

Accept the way God does things, for who can straighten what He has made crooked? Enjoy prosperity while you can, but when hard times strike, realize that both come from God. Remember that nothing is certain in this life.

- - - - - - - - - - - - - - - - - - - -

Anything resembling prosperity in my life has come from God, and when times get hard, God is also in them. Whether he created the hard times or allowed them, only he knows. But what I do know is that he is always there for me no matter what.

God is sovereign with unlimited power and authority. He is exalted, supreme, and unlimited in extent. He knows exactly what I need and knows when to provide it. He uplifts and encourages me!

- - - - - - - - - - - - - - - - - - - -

Psalm 115:3
Our God is in the heavens, and He does as He wishes.

- - - - - - - - - - - - - - - - - - - -

What is there in this world that we can be absolutely certain about? Anything?

How is it that the sovereign Almighty God loves us and cares about us? It is beyond any understanding, and that is where faith comes in.

- - - - - - - - - - - - - - - - - - - -

Hebrews 11:6
And it is impossible to please God without faith. Anyone who wants to come to Him must believe that God exists and that He rewards those who sincerely seek Him.

- - - - - - - - - - - - - - - - - - - -

We were discussing lessons learned from unemployment one day when my sister-in-law Vickie wisely said, *true freedom is not in what we have, but in what we do not need.* At first it seems like a contradiction. But it's not. It is truth.

Once you decide to think about what you do not need instead of thinking about what you have or how to get more, what's important comes into focus.

We have so much that we do not need that we become oblivious to the fact that it is a blessing and not a requirement.

How do we distinguish between wants and needs in life? Helen Keller put it so well when she said that many people have a wrong idea of what constitutes true happiness. It is not attached through self-gratification but through fidelity to a worthy purpose.

- - - - - - - - - - - - - - - - - -

Isaiah 41:10
Don't be afraid, for I am with you.
Don't be discouraged for I am your God.
I will strengthen you and help you.
I will hold you up with my victorious right hand.

- - - - - - - - - - - - - - - - - -

Fear of Failure. Does anyone not have that fear?

- - - - - - - - - - - - - - - - - -

Our greatest fear should not be of failure but of succeeding at things in life that don't really matter.
~ Francis Chan[xxxiii]

- - - - - - - - - - - - - - - - - -

Have you thought about what you do in terms of whether or not it matters?

I ask myself every morning, "What am I doing today that will matter in 5 years? Or for eternity?" If I wait until the end of the day to think about that, there are many days that I am ashamed of the time I wasted.

* * *

Personal Challenge:

What do you need to surrender?

Write down what you need and then step back and think about it – is it really something you need or just something you want?

- -

- -

- -

- -

- -

* * *

Chapter 7: Preparation

- - - - - - - - - - - - - - - - - - - -

Learning is not compulsory...
neither is survival.
~ W. Edwards Deming[xxxiv]

- - - - - - - - - - - - - - - - - - - -

How can we thrive while we on this journey or do we merely hope to survive?

This Accidental Sabbatical has provided me with the best opportunity to prepare and to learn new things. I have more time and mental space available than I have had in years!

One woman I met said that since she had been laid off, she could not deal with anything and was spending her time lying in bed, reading romance novels with her kitty wrapped around her feet.

That is denial, not survival.

Surviving is important. Thriving even more so.

What is God preparing for me? I definitely believe that he knows what is next and is preparing me for it.

- -

Jeremiah 1:5 NIV
Before I formed you in the womb I knew you, before
you were born I set you apart.

- -

Max DePree says in his book Leadership Is an Art: In the end, it is important to remember that we cannot become what we need to be, by remaining what we are.

- -

Often what seems like an impossible climb is just a
staircase without the steps drawn in.
~ Robert Brault[xxxv]

- -

Close your eyes.

Visualize a staircase with no steps drawn in.

As I do this exercise, I ask myself, what am I doing to find those steps on the staircase?

Am I using this sabbatical effectively to make myself better? How?

Here is what I am doing:

Studying and reading the unread books I have gathered over the years that pepper my bookshelves. I am taking free courses, both online and at the local community college; courses on Leadership, Organizations, Behavior, Business Models, and others.

Seeking out and meeting people whose expertise and experience is different from mine. We share information and encourage one another.

Volunteering my skills to non-profit organizations and helping other job seekers create resumes. I am using what I have to give now while I am learning more.

No one stands still.

We are either moving forward or slipping backward.

You have to get started to move forward.

- - - - - - - - - - - - - - - - - - -

Ecclesiastes 11:4 LB
If you wait for perfect conditions, you will never get anything done.

- - - - - - - - - - - - - - - - - - -

Are you moving forward, figuring out your passion or what is worthy of your effort?

What you can do in this life to make a difference?

Are you being honest with yourself?

What are you busy doing?

As Jim Rohn wisely says, Don't mistake movement for achievement. It's easy to get faked out by being busy. The question is, Busy doing what?

* * *

What are you doing today that will matter in 5 years?

Or for eternity?

Asking myself that question keeps my focus on the present – just today. I do not focus on the past that I cannot change, or on the future that has not yet arrived and may never arrive.

I try to do what it says here in Ecclesiastes…

– –

Ecclesiastes 11:6
Plant your seed in the morning and keep busy all afternoon, for you don't know if profit will come from one activity or another – or maybe both.

– –

I plant my seeds every morning and stay productive until the end of the workday. I have created a work schedule for myself from 7am to 5pm on most days. Just like in a 'regular' job, during this Accidental Sabbatical I manage my time by keeping a weekly calendar, a To Do list and a schedule for each day. After many years of consulting, in order to track project time, I keep a notebook – a time journal - at the right of my mouse pad where I document what I do and how long it takes. This is a visual reminder for me that I am moving in the right direction or that I am stalled and wasting time.

This is not a step by step 'how-to' guide for anyone to follow exactly… but it is what I do. If it helps, use it as an outline of strategy that you adopt or modify for yourself.

Drinking my morning coffee, I begin with what I call HGQT – Higher Ground Quality Time. I have no idea where I got the name… it has been the acronym in my journal for so long I've forgotten. Others might call it prayer and meditation. For me this time includes reading Scriptures. Praying. Reading devotionals. Keeping track of what input I allow into my brain and the resulting attitude, because the two definitely go together.

Then I check for emails from friends or family, the "real emails". After that I check the many email alerts I receive daily for new job postings and scan the opportunities. In the beginning months of this journey I spent several hours of the day searching online job postings. And while I still scan the job boards, networking and intentional communication with people is now a more effective way to search in this job market. Or so the experts say. So I practice it.

Intentional communication includes attending job seeker networking meetings or networking at luncheons with local meet-up groups. (Specifics on these are in the Resources section). It also means developing new friendships, contacting old friends and former colleagues and letting them know I am looking for a new job, the goal being to simply inform, not to intrude on their time.

I have actually not met one person who was hired because of who they knew, although the experts say that's how it is done. I know jobs are found online and I don't discount any idea or method. There is no science to this process and certainly no magic bullet.

But I digress...

In this season of preparation, every seed planted is growing something. What seeds am I planting in my brain?

Asking myself this question keeps me cognizant of the importance of the content input. Whose words am I reading? What blogs fill my brain and what are their messages? What music do I listen to? What shows or movies do I watch? Am I aware of what I am planting in my brain?

I take classes. Massive Open Online Courses (MOOC's) are offered free online. The ability to acquire knowledge in several different subjects is available to anyone with an Internet connection or a Smartphone, without regard for physical location or financial condition. All that is required is that we sign up, show up and do the work.

I am doing my part in preparing myself for whatever God has in mind, whenever he brings it into my life. Because I believe that Benjamin Franklin was right when he said that if I fail to prepare, I prepare to fail.

- - - - - - - - - - - - - - - - - - - -

Proverbs 24:27
Do your planning and prepare your fields before building your house.

- - - - - - - - - - - - - - - - - - - -

Is there anything in your life that is limiting your future? Are you striving to be your best and do you continually work to improve yourself? I think it is important to do that for many reasons. It helps maintain sanity, gives us a purpose for each day, teaches us new skills and introduces us to new thinking.

* * *

- - - - - - - - - - - - - - - - - -

1 Corinthians 9:25-27 (NIV)
Everyone who competes in the games goes into strict
training. They do it to get a crown that will not last,
but we do it to get a crown that will last forever.
Therefore I do not run like someone running
aimlessly; I do not fight like a boxer beating the air.
No, I strike a blow to my body and make it my slave
so that after I have preached to others, I myself will
not be disqualified for the prize.

- - - - - - - - - - - - - - - - - -

The Winter Olympics have recently concluded; they always inspire me. I am not an athlete by any means. What draws me to watch each competition is the total dedication of the athletes. As spectators we see brief minutes of their talent and the outcome of their hard work. Only the athletes and their coaches know the sacrifices required and the training needed to even compete at the Olympic level. Yet they inspire me with their commitment and it pushes me to strive for excellence in all areas.

What can we learn from them?

We know that they have developed the habit of excellence and they have an overwhelming belief that nothing will stop them from winning. Their excellence is an attitude propelling them to victory.

I keep working on it! I know it is all about developing the habits that will make me prepared when an opportunity shows up. Even as the weeks and months go on, I know there will always be something new to learn, something to give me a sense of significance and accomplishment.

* * *

Personal challenge:

What specific things are you doing to prepare?

What can you do today to help someone else prepare?

_ _

_ _

_ _

_ _

_ _

* * *

Chapter 8: Perseverance

- - - - - - - - - - - - - - - - - - - -

2 Corinthians 4:7-9

We now have this light shining in our hearts, but we ourselves are like fragile clay jars containing this great treasure. This makes it clear that our great power is from God, not from ourselves. We are pressed on every side by troubles but we are not crushed. We are perplexed, but not driven to despair. We are hunted down, but never abandoned by God. We get knocked down, but we are not destroyed.

- - - - - - - - - - - - - - - - - - - -

I keep looking with eternal hope. Not just searching for a job or a paycheck, but for work that will be a passion for me. Is that unrealistic?

Will I have to just settle?

As of today I have applied for 236 positions (I keep track in a spreadsheet of job search data).

Of those I have had somewhere around 36 interviews.

That does not take into consideration the panel interviews which include time spent with an HR person and then multiple department managers, all in one interview. Nor does it include short informational interviews some people have given when asked.

It is so easy to doubt myself and to feel disrespected when they don't take 30 seconds or so to send me an email about the status of a position, or to respond to mine when I follow up. Then I remember that maybe it has nothing to do with me at all. What if they don't want to have that conversation? What if they worry that talking about it might backfire on them somehow? This is what HR people indicate is the issue. However to me it just feels like rudeness.

There are times I feel like I'm 14 all over again, trying to find a friend, looking for a group where I might belong, repeatedly rejected.

And then another surge of hope will come. Whenever I do get a response or actually end up with an interview, God confirms again that he still sees what is going on in my life and is taking care of it. I had a moment of hope like that yesterday when I got a call setting up an interview for this afternoon. Even as I wait, I have peace that God will give me favor with them, and if it's the next assignment, that he will make it clear to both of us.

* * *

Simon Sinek says: Working hard for something we don't care about is called stress; working hard for something we love is called passion. I am a very hard worker and I definitely choose passion over stress.

Dear Lord, please lead me to the work that ignites my passion.

Anne Lamott wrote in *Bird by Bird* (my favorite book on writing):

I heard a preacher say recently that hope is a revolutionary patience; let me add that so is being a writer. Hope begins in the dark, the stubborn hope that if you just show up and try to do the right thing, the dawn will come. You wait and watch and work: you don't give up.

That same hope applies to looking for a job as well. This Accidental Sabbatical is not a quick turnaround, at least not for anyone I have met on the journey. In fact, some people have just given up. They are long past collecting unemployment, they have had it with rejection. Some people are retraining for new careers but some others have just quit.

Did they quit too soon?

Was a miracle right around the corner?

- - - - - - - - - - - - - - - - - - - -

2 Corinthians 4:16 (MSG)
We're not giving up. How could we! Even though on the outside it often looks like things are falling apart on us, on the inside, where God is making new life, not a day goes by without his unfolding grace.

- - - - - - - - - - - - - - - - - - - -

Don't quit!

Keep believing that something will happen eventually. I say that to myself as well, not just to you.

– – – – – – – – – – – – – – – – – – –

Keep scribbling! Something will happen.
~ Frank McCourt[xxxvi]

– – – – – – – – – – – – – – – – – – –

More than twenty years ago I started writing a book. It began as a sort of therapeutic exercise for me as I healed after being released from an abusive marriage. As I wrote, it became something I knew I could share with others... that somewhere out there was another woman, or man, in an abusive relationship who needed to see that release was possible and that grace can win. So I kept working on it and polishing it and rewriting some more.

One day during this Accidental Sabbatical it occurred to me that I had no excuse not to finish it now, and that maybe finishing the book was my next assignment. After all, I am constantly writing something; it has always been a passion of mine. And although I know most writers will say it is not a lucrative way to make a living, if at all, I figured I had no excuse not to try. So I scheduled time every day to work on the book, and I got it finished.

Released: A True Story of Escape from an Abusive Marriage, is published now and it is helping people. I know it is because I have heard from some of them. No amount of money or career ladder-climbing could provide the joy I have in knowing that sharing my story has made a difference in someone's life.

Have you figured out your passion?

I have heard that to figure out your passion, think about what you do for free. John Wooden said, *Do not let what you cannot do interfere with what you can do.*

While there are probably thousands of words of wisdom to encourage perseverance during struggle, these, in particular, have encouraged me on more than one level during this time when I need daily encouragement just to keep going. I often pull these quotes out of my Hope Box and read them out loud.

- - - - - - - - - - - - - - - - - -

Never give up on a dream just because of the time it will take to accomplish it. The time will pass anyway.
~ Earl Nightingale[xxxvii]

- - - - - - - - - - - - - - - - - -

Talent is cheaper than table salt. What separates the talented individual from the successful one is a lot of hard work.
~ Stephen King[xxxviii]

- - - - - - - - - - - - - - - - - -

Success is to be measured not so much by the position that one has reached in life as by the obstacles which he has overcome.
~ Booker T Washington[xxxix]

- - - - - - - - - - - - - - - - - -

I will persist until I succeed. Always will I take another step. If that is of no avail I will take another, and yet another. In truth, one step at a time is not too difficult... I know that small attempts, repeated, will complete any undertaking.
~ Og Mandino[xl]

– – – – – – – – – – – – – – – – – – –

Don't worry about failures, worry about the chances you miss when you don't even try.
~ Jack Canfield[xli]

– – – – – – – – – – – – – – – – – – –

My great concern is not whether you have failed, but whether you are content with your failure.
~ Abraham Lincoln[xlii]

– – – – – – – – – – – – – – – – – – –

* * *

Personal challenge:

What is your passion?

If you don't know yet, what would you do for free?

– – – – – – – – – – – – – – – – – – – –

– – – – – – – – – – – – – – – – – – – –

– – – – – – – – – – – – – – – – – – – –

– – – – – – – – – – – – – – – – – – – –

– – – – – – – – – – – – – – – – – – – –

– – – – – – – – – – – – – – – – – – – –

It always helps you to help others... what will you do today to help someone else persevere?

----

* * *

Chapter 9: Control

God is in control. My hope is in him.

He is God. I am not.

I repeat this to myself. Every. Day.

I don't like feeling that I am not in control.

- - - - - - - - - - - - - - - - - - - -

Psalm 23:4

Even though I walk through the darkest valley, I will not be afraid, for You are close beside me. Your rod and Your staff protect and comfort me.

- - - - - - - - - - - - - - - - - - - -

It often feels like I am walking through a dark tunnel because I see no end in sight. So I have to hold on to the truth that God is in control, leading me through the tunnel, and because he is, I know all is right with my world. If it doesn't feel like it, that doesn't matter. It's faith. Especially when it doesn't make sense.

Actually do we need to have faith when it does make sense?

- - - - - - - - - - - - - - - - - - - -

Proverbs 3:5
Trust in the Lord with all your heart; do not depend
on your own understanding.

- - - - - - - - - - - - - - - - - - - -

Os Hillman, in his TGIF devotional, quoted Watchman
Nee on the subject of relying on our own human strength:

- - - - - - - - - - - - - - - - - - - -

I believe many people are so rich and strong that they
give no ground for God to work. I frequently recall
the words, "helpless and hopeless." I must tell God,
"all that I have is Yours, I myself have nothing. Apart
from You I am truly helpless and hopeless." We need
to have such a dependent attitude toward God that it
is as if we cannot inhale or exhale without Him. In
this way we shall see that our power as well as our
holiness all comes from Him. Oh how God delights in
seeing us coming hopeless and helpless to Him.
~ Watchman Nee[xliii]

- - - - - - - - - - - - - - - - - - - -

There may be some people who would use that as an
excuse to determine that they don't have to do anything but
just sit around and wait for God to push them where he wants
them; that instead of doing the work they can just lie around
and something will magically come to them. It never happens
that way.

You reap what you sow. Always.

- - - - - - - - - - - - - - - - - - -

Galatians 6:7-9 (MSG)
Don't be misled: No one makes a fool of God. What a
person plants, he will harvest. The person who plants
selfishness, ignoring the needs of others – ignoring
God! – harvests a crop of weeds. All he'll have to
show for his life is weeds! But the one who plants in
response to God, letting God's Spirit do the growth
work in him, harvests a crop of real life, eternal life.
So let's not allow ourselves to get fatigued doing
good. At the right time we will harvest a good crop if
we don't give up, or quit.

- - - - - - - - - - - - - - - - - - -

If you have ever planted a garden, you know that it is an absolute fact that what you plant is what will grow.

Pete Wilson recently wrote[xliv]: It's an agricultural reality. If you plant tomato seeds in your seedling tray, guess what you get? That's right, tomatoes. Every. Single. Time.

That same principle applies to the seeds that we plant in our brains. We must be intentional in our thoughts as well as our actions.

Deliberately plant truth and excellence.

I guarantee that replacing negative thoughts with positive ones will change the way you think. In fact, I learned in a leadership class that positivity *changes* the cellular structure of the brain.

－ － － － － － － － － － － － － － － － － －

Philippians 4:8
Fix your thoughts on what is true, and honorable,
and right, and pure, and lovely, and admirable. Think
about things that are excellent and worthy of praise.

－ － － － － － － － － － － － － － － － － －

Remember, the thoughts that you think and the
statements you make regarding yourself determine
your mental attitude. If you have a worthwhile
objective, find the one reason why you can achieve it
rather than hundreds of reasons why you can't.
~ Napoleon Hill[xlv]

－ － － － － － － － － － － － － － － － －

What do you think about every day?
How do you talk to yourself?

－ － － － － － － － － － － － － － － － －

Colossians 3:1-2
Since you have been raised to new life with Christ, set
your sights on the realities of heaven, where Christ
sits in the place of honor at God's right hand. Think
about the things of heaven, not the things of earth.

－ － － － － － － － － － － － － － － － －

When I was raising my son, the word 'stupid' was
forbidden in our house. If you called yourself stupid, you had
to stop and immediately apologize to yourself for it.
Occasionally I find myself doing the same thing, walking

around the house in a bad self-talk mode, and I apologize. Out loud. To myself. Shad Helmstetter's book on Self-Talk (on the book list) is an excellent resource on this subject.

- - - - - - - - - - - - - - - - - - -

Exodus 15:2
The Lord is my strength and my song; He has given me victory. This is my God, and I will praise Him – my father's God, and I will exalt Him.

- - - - - - - - - - - - - - - - - - -

It is tempting at times to just settle for something, anything, even when I know it is less than what I am capable of doing. There is a delicate balance between being willing to do whatever work is given to me, and just settling for whatever comes along. That temptation rears its head especially when I am impatient and forget that I am depending on God. Or when I want to be done with waiting, and instead try to solve my problems my own way.

Again, I have to remind myself every day that he is my hope and my strength and he will lead me to what He wants for me, even if I have no idea what it will be or when it will happen. I want to know his will and wait for it.

- - - - - - - - - - - - - - - - - - -

I can say from experience that 95% of knowing the will of God consists in being prepared to do it before you know what it is.
~ Donald Grey Barnhouse[xlvi]

If 'reminding myself every day' seems to be a repetitive pattern here, it is.

Since this is a career transition – whatever that means for each of us individually – it is possible that God's hand is directing us down a completely different road in life. I believe he is in my life.

I know that, a) there is no perfect job out there and b) I must grow anywhere that I am planted. And since I am planted in this Accidental Sabbatical right now, I have to grow here or I will not survive. If I don't grow, I cannot thrive. And that certainly would not that lead me to a new position.

* * *

So how do I find the elusive will of God in my life?

Well, I definitely know it is **not** his will when it is something that does not follow the instruction in his Word and his prompting in my heart. That might sound like reverse engineering, and in reality, it is sort of a process of elimination. If there is any question of absolute integrity, it is most definitely not his will. Remove any possibility that will not bring glory to God and you are on the right track.

God-given dreams will never require you to abandon God-given values. ~ Pete Wilson
(Crosspoint Community Church Facebook post)

Would you walk away from a job offer? Have you?

- - - - - - - - - - - - - - - - - - - -

Sometimes walking away has nothing do with weakness, and everything to do with strength. We walk away not because we want others to realize our worth and value, but because we finally realize our own. ~ Unknown

- - - - - - - - - - - - - - - - - - - -

What if it challenged your integrity, or worse, compromised it completely? Especially if it was a job with the promise of a lot of money that required you to compromise your ethics? Don't do it! As Tom Peters says, *There is no such thing as a minor lapse in integrity.*

- - - - - - - - - - - - - - - - - - - -

Character is like a tree, and reputation like a shadow. The shadow is what we think of it; the tree is the real thing.
~ Abraham Lincoln[xlvii]

- - - - - - - - - - - - - - - - - - - -

Justin Davis tweeted this: Don't allow the thrill of "what's next" (to) cause you to miss the significance of "what's now".

Based on the book that Justin and his wife Trish recently wrote, *Beyond Ordinary: When a Good Marriage Just Isn't Good Enough,* it is likely he makes that statement in the context of relationship. But as I read his tweet, I think of many other scenarios as well.

My husband and I have gone through different seasons in our marriage, and there have been times when I didn't realize it would be just a season. All I knew at the time was that things were changing and not by my choice.

As my son was growing up I knew that I had to treasure each stage, knowing that each was a season that would happen only once and be over far too quickly.

That truth about "what's next" and "what's now" applies to this Accidental Sabbatical as well.

This is a significant time in my life, and while at some point there will be the thrill of something next, I don't want to squander the significance of what is happening now as I wait.

I commit to not missing the significance of now.

- -

Isaiah 60:22B EXB
I am the Lord, and when it is time, I will make these
things happen quickly.

- -

I fully accept that this Accidental Sabbatical is God's plan for my life at this time. Why? And for how long? I will know in time.

I continually search for the lessons that God has for me here and now. I refuse to get ahead of him and think I've figured it out on my own. This season is not mine to control.

He is God. I am not.

- -

Don't ask God what He wants you to do and then decide to say yes. Start with yes, and then God will tell you what to do. ~ Rick Warren

— — — — — — — — — — — — — — — — — — —

Personal challenge:

What do you do when you feel out of control?

What will you do today to help someone else who is struggling with feeling out of control?

— — — — — — — — — — — — — — — — — — — —

— — — — — — — — — — — — — — — — — — — —

— — — — — — — — — — — — — — — — — — — —

— — — — — — — — — — — — — — — — — — — —

— — — — — — — — — — — — — — — — — — — —

* * *

Chapter 10: Provision

- - - - - - - - - - - - - - - - - -

Smile every chance you get. Not because life has been easy, perfect, or exactly as you had anticipated, but because you choose to be happy and grateful for all the good things you do have and all the problems you know you don't have. ~ Unknown

- - - - - - - - - - - - - - - - - -

How can I lose hope when I am blessed every day?

I am counting my blessings every day! I have a spreadsheet called my "Book of Blessings" where I keep a record of the both the major and the minor things. I brainstorm for ways to be thankful. I journal in a stream of conscious manner, focusing on blessings.

Some things may seem insignificant, but what seems inconsequential to me today may be significant on another day. I count them all. Choosing to live with gratitude is what brings me to a state of happiness.

As Ralph Waldo Emerson wrote in the 1800's: Cultivate the habit of being grateful for every good thing that comes to you, and to give thanks continuously. And because all things have contributed to your advancement, you should include all things in your gratitude.

Call it a Gratitude Journal.

Call it a Blessings List.

Call it whatever you want but write down everything that blesses you.

- -

Gratitude is not only the greatest of virtues, but the parent of all others. ~ Marcus Tullius Cicero[xlviii]

- -

During this Accidental Sabbatical I am blessed to...

... be in a peaceful and quiet environment. Every. Day.

... have time to pray; to do more than say 'hi' in passing to the Almighty God. Every. Day.

... have time and energy to focus on my husband's needs and to search for ways to serve and bless him. Every. Day.

... have time to focus on, pray for my family. Every. Day.

... have a roof over my head, "food with my meals", and good health.

... be able to help others

... be able to avoid rush hour traffic most of the time!

What is a blessing to you?

When I do this exercise, I stay hopeful about my situation and constantly look for blessings. In everything.

Keeping track of my blessings is the primary activity that will guarantee a changed attitude in me.

I see God's hand; he has provided everything I need.

– – – – – – – – – – – – – – – – – – – –

Ephesians 1:3
All praise to God, the Father of our Lord Jesus Christ,
who has blessed us with every spiritual blessing in
the heavenly realms because we are united with
Christ.

– – – – – – – – – – – – – – – – – – –

Gratitude is powerful.
There is always something for which to be thankful.
Always.

– – – – – – – – – – – – – – – – – – –

Often, in the midst of great problems, we stop short of
the real blessing God has for us, which is a fresh
vision of who He is.
~ Anne Graham Lotz[xlix]

– – – – – – – – – – – – – – – – – – –

Isaiah 58:11
The Lord will guide you continually, giving you
water when you are dry and restoring your strength.
You will be like a well-watered garden, like an ever-
flowing spring.

– – – – – – – – – – – – – – – – – – –

I totally reframe my world and feel restored when I focus
on gratitude. Likewise, I am guaranteed to lose that feeling if I

focus on someone else's blessings instead of my own. I have what God wants me to have and knows I need.

– – – – – – – – – – – – – – – – – – –

Hebrews 11:3
By faith we understand that the entire universe was formed at God's command, so that what we now see did not come from anything that can be seen.

– – – – – – – – – – – – – – – – – – –

The holidays typically slow down the hiring process, even grinding it to a complete halt. So for the months of November and December, I give myself a vacation from the job hunt. Being unemployed only means we don't have a paying job; we still go to work every day, searching, networking, and praying. So especially during that time off, I focus on every good thing and have a relaxed holiday enjoying my blessings.

– – – – – – – – – – – – – – – – – – –

Once you discover that you can, then you must. And it's not easy. You have to take direct steps. You really have to count your blessings and you have to make a decided effort to not get seduced by the blues.
~ Al Jarreau[1]

– – – – – – – – – – – – – – – – – – –

What I think about and where I keep my focus is a choice, a decision I make daily.

– – – – – – – – – – – – – – – – – – –

Philippians 2:5
You must have the same attitude that Christ Jesus
had.

— — — — — — — — — — — — — — — — —

When I read this scripture telling me to have the same attitude as Jesus, I know the only way it is possible is if I let him live through me. I understand that he is my provision for everything, including an attitude like his. We choose to have a great attitude.

Every day we have that choice. We can look at what we do have, or what we do not have. When we choose the positive and share your joy, we provide encouragement to others. One friend told me that my positive emails encouraging him to be optimistic and choose joy made him feel worse. I can't 'make him' feel anything though; all I can do is spread positivity and hope it is contagious.

— — — — — — — — — — — — — — — — —

Psalm 126:3-6
Yes, the Lord has done amazing things for us! What joy! Restore our fortunes, Lord, as streams renew the desert. Those who plant in tears will harvest with shouts of joy. They weep as they go to plant their seed, but they sing as they return with the harvest.

— — — — — — — — — — — — — — — — —

I have never been without shelter and at least some food. There were times I was hungry, but I have always had something to eat. God promises to take care of my needs. Not everything I want, but always what I need. I have seen his faithfulness multiple times in my life. God has always provided. Our four years in Florida in our 'poor college students' season left me with a totally new understanding of the depth of His provision.

I know God will provide not just what we need materially, but he also provides for my psychological needs, regularly renewing my faith and hope during this Accident Sabbatical. I am thankful for that every day.

There is huge uncertainty in this season, from both a financial perspective and a career perspective, as it has been in other seasons of my life.

Often I wonder, am I done working forever? Will I ever have another paycheck? But even as I pray those words out loud, I know that each day may be wrapped in pleasure or pain, or sometimes both, but without pain, how would I know and appreciate pleasure?

It is all good because God is good and he has it under control.

I know that one day this season will be only a memory and then I will truly know the value of all of these moments. God provides for our needs every day and he will provide the next assignment in His time.

Until then, I just show up for the doors he opens.

- - - - - - - - - - - - - - - - - -

Exodus 23:20

See, I am sending an angel before you to protect you on your journey and lead you safely to the place I have prepared for you.

- - - - - - - - - - - - - - - - - -

I believe that he has prepared a place for me and that he is protecting me on this journey. My greatest blessing is God's love and his promise that every day of my future is with him. I believe that promise!

What better blessing could there be?

- - - - - - - - - - - - - - - - - -

Psalm 18:30

God's way is perfect. All the Lord's promises prove true. He is a shield for all who look to him for protection.

- - - - - - - - - - - - - - - - - -

Personal challenge:

Focus on your blessings!

Write them down! Big or small!

- - - - - - - - - - - - - - - - - - - -

- - - - - - - - - - - - - - - - - - - -

- - - - - - - - - - - - - - - - - - - -

- - - - - - - - - - - - - - - - - - - -

- - - - - - - - - - - - - - - - - - - -

★ ★ ★

Chapter 11: Self-Esteem

- - - - - - - - - - - - - - - - - - -

There is only one way to avoid criticism: do nothing,
say nothing and be nothing.
~ Elbert Hubbard[li]

- - - - - - - - - - - - - - - - - -

Maintaining hope is critical to my psyche and self-esteem. Keeping my self-esteem high has been one of the most difficult parts of this journey for me, maybe even more difficult than losing the income.

In nearly every interview I feel judged on some level, and usually by hiring managers or recruiters with far less knowledge, experience and skill than I have. Yet, I am at their mercy. We all are. And even when I feel that an interview has gone extremely well, when there is no feedback or response when I follow up, it is easy to feel invisible. Unwanted. Insignificant.

It happens to other people too from what I hear. One friend described herself as 'broke and broken'. Literally millions of people are in this same situation, on an Accidental Sabbatical that may have felt like a vacation at first, until it didn't end when planned. There are many more of us than the 'official' unemployment numbers state. I, for one, have never been included in those numbers since I never collected any unemployment compensation or any other government subsidy.

Those tempting pity parties lure me, especially on a day when nothing good happens. But they accomplish nothing. It is a conscious decision every day to stay positive and not beat up on myself.

What are your triggers? Do you know what causes your self-esteem to spiral down?

The way I stay positive is to focus on Jesus. If I focus on a job – trying to find *the* job - then I put my faith in myself.

- - - - - - - - - - - - - - - - - -

Hebrews 12:2
We do this by keeping our eyes on Jesus, the champion who initiates and perfects our faith. Because of the joy awaiting Him, He endured the cross, disregarding its shame. Now He is seated in the place of honor beside God's throne.

- - - - - - - - - - - - - - - - - -

If I think about the fact that I am looking for the Lord's next assignment, I can wait peacefully until He places me.

I promise I did not pray for more patience! However it is apparently a lesson I am destined to learn repeatedly in life.

I have met so many others on their own Accidental Sabbatical, in various stages of it. Some are distraught, some relieved, positive, and all of us are trying to stay sane as we struggle with our identity.

We struggle with who we are, what to be.

We struggle with what to do.

We struggle with feeling that we now have nowhere to belong.

Too often we identify ourselves through our jobs. Think about it. When was the last time you met someone who said, "tell me about you, what do you read, what do you cook, what are your hobbies?"

No. Instead they ask, "so what do you do for a living?" or "where do you work?"

When we are working, we find a sense of belonging in our company and with our colleagues. Whether we were part of a team, or a department, we all worked somewhere and we felt we belonged, perhaps even felt significance. We had employee numbers and badges with our names on them that allowed us entry into the building. Maybe even a nameplate hanging on our office door or cubicle.

For some people, colleagues and coworkers are family, or the relationships become like family. And too many of us have spent more time with our work family than with our own at home.

* * *

Then there is the interview process, where it sometimes feels like I have a sign on my back announcing my insecurities. How do we express interest and even passion about a position without sounding desperate? And when we don't sound desperate is it only because we have practiced our lines, and rehearsed our answers and tone of voice?

How can we keep these insecurities at bay?

The trend now in hiring is the behavioral interview. Perhaps you have experienced this type of interview where you are asked a series of questions about how you behaved in a particular situation, questions designed to reveal personality strengths and weaknesses, and cultural fit, among other things.

These are some of the questions I have been asked:

- Describe a specific time when you had to deal with an angry coworker? How did you respond and how did you resolve it?
- Tell us about a time when you failed and how you dealt with it?
- Describe a significant change that occurred in your job and how you adapted to that change?
- Give me a specific example of a time when you …

And the questions go on and on. There is a document being circulated entitled "The 64 Toughest Interview Questions" and there are several websites that offer examples of how to answer the questions. Search for it online and answer them when you are preparing for an interview. It is great practice.

I am sure I am not the only one to have learned the importance of thinking about what story is the best one to tell and then rehearsing out loud before an interview.

I don't consider myself a prideful person, nor do I even respect egotistical people, so it is difficult for me to brag about myself or my accomplishments. Therefore, when these questions require me to do so, I try to remember what my customers or managers have said about me to use as examples.

When I am nervous about what I will say in an interview, and whether or not I will communicate properly, I pray and I remember Moses and this conversation he had with God:

– –

Exodus 4:10-12
But Moses pleaded with the LORD, "O Lord, I'm not
very good with words. I never have been, and I'm not
now, even though You have spoken to me. I get
tongue-tied, and my words get tangled."
Then the LORD asked Moses, "Who makes a person's
mouth? Who decides whether people speak or do not
speak, hear or do not hear, see or do not see? Is it not
I, the LORD? Now go! I will be with you as you
speak, and I will instruct you in what to say.

– –

I love that! And God kept his promise. Some may not believe that God will give us the words we need to say in an interview, but I know from experience that he does. More than once he has brought to mind a specific story that I hadn't thought of in advance.

I also firmly believe that if we do not get the job, we were not meant to be there.

I repeat, if I did not get the job, I was not meant to get it and that is a *good* thing.

Being hired or not may have nothing at all to do with you or me. It may be that an internal candidate was always going to get the position and protocol required that they interview more than one person. It may be that there is not even an opening at the time and they are only collecting resumes for the future.

In one interview I had, after 4 hours of meeting with multiple managers, I asked the last manager point blank if there was a current opening. He admitted there was no position actually open at that time.

I was not happy and felt defeated once again. I had spent many days preparing for the interview and I knew I had done well. I had put myself at their mercy, encountered intensive grilling and up until that point really thought I might have a chance. I had also invested about three gallons of gas. As I drove home from the long interview, I called my husband and said "I just want to talk to someone who loves me."

As time passed, I saw with regularity that this company had job postings for the same position around the beginning of each new quarter, giving a clear indication of high turnover and an expectation of unmet quotas. I've seen this with several companies actually.

It is not always about you at all.

On days when my self-esteem feels particularly battered, I go through the truths in my Hope Box and read. I have confidence knowing that I can choose how I feel, no matter the circumstance, even if I cannot change the situation.

- - - - - - - - - - - - - - - - - - - -

You wouldn't worry so much about what others think of you if you realized how seldom they do.
~ Eleanor Roosevelt[lii]

- - - - - - - - - - - - - - - - - - - -

We need to remind each other that the cup of sorrow is also the cup of joy, that precisely what causes us sadness can become the fertile ground for gladness.
~ Henri Nouwen[liii]

- - - - - - - - - - - - - - - - - - - -

The hunger for love is much more difficult to remove than the hunger for bread.
~ Mother Teresa[liv]

- - - - - - - - - - - - - - - - - - - -

This verse in Colossians is my career life verse:

- - - - - - - - - - - - - - - - - - - -

Colossians 3:23
Work willingly at whatever you do, as though you were working for the Lord rather than for people.

- - - - - - - - - - - - - - - - - - - -

Accidental Sabbatical

In this sabbatical season I have to focus on who I *am*, not what I *do* as I learn how to *be*.

* * *

Personal challenge:

What triggers cause you to feel beaten up?

What actions help restore your high self-esteem?

What can you do to help someone else's self-esteem?

- -

- -

- -

- -

- -

* * *

Chapter 12: Significance

We may not all hope to change the world, but we all want meaning in our lives.

You are significant, with or without a job.

Read it again. Say it out loud: "I am significant, with or without a job."

You are impacting people whether or not you realize it. A simple smile, an encouraging word, saying thank you to someone, are all ways in which you are making a difference.

I struggle some days more than others, feeling unimportant without any problems to solve. I have had customer-facing roles for so many years that I miss interacting with people on the phone and by email to discover their needs and figure out solutions to meet them. With no one to help, and no problem to solve, I feel insignificant at times.

So I have to remember that my significance is not defined by my work, that a simple gesture of thanking the butcher at the grocery store for giving me a great cut of meat can make his day. Or I can send an email or a personal note and encourage a fellow job-hunter who is feeling lost and hopeless on this journey. I often spend way too many hours looking for jobs for other people instead of myself.

- - - - - - - - - - - - - - - - - - -

A smile costs nothing, but creates much good. It enriches those who receive it without impoverishing those who give it away. It happens in a flash, but the memory of it can last forever. No one is so rich that he can get along without it. No one is too poor to feel rich when receiving it. It is rest to the weary, daylight to the discouraged, sunshine to the sad and nature's best anecdote for trouble. Yet it cannot be bought, begged, borrowed or stolen.
~ Adrian Rogers[lv]

- - - - - - - - - - - - - - - - - - -

1 Corinthians 15:58
So my dear brothers and sisters, be strong and immovable. Always work enthusiastically for the Lord, for you know that nothing you do for the Lord is ever useless.

- - - - - - - - - - - - - - - - - - -

Then one thing leads to another as people you help in turn help someone else. You know how the 'pay it forward' phenomenon works. It is real.

- - - - - - - - - - - - - - - - - - -

Our souls are not hungry for fame, comfort, wealth or power. Those rewards create almost as many

problems as they solve. Our souls are hungry for meaning, for the sense that we have figured out how to live so that our lives matter, so that the world will be at least a little bit different for our having passed through it.
~ Rabbi Harold Kushner[lvi]

- - - - - - - - - - - - - - - - - - -

Psalm 69:32
The humble will see their God at work and be glad.
Let all who seek God's help be encouraged.

- - - - - - - - - - - - - - - - - - -

Some days I wake up and ask myself, what can I do differently today? Actually many days start that way. So I create routines that give me a sense of order and structure in an otherwise structure-less day ahead of me.

I can get caught up in the 'what ifs' and ruin my mood, and waste hours of time. I have to monitor that self-talk and guard my thoughts. Once it gets sour, it is tough to pull it back.

I cannot fix anything in the past. Not the long term past and not even the past that was yesterday. I have only today.

So what can I do today that will help me discover how God wants to use me today?

I often journal to get the thoughts out of my head. As I journal, I think about what makes me passionate... what makes me feel alive. How can I find more of that today?

What is your passion? What will you do today that will make you feel significant? Who will you impact today?

As Maya Angelou famously reminded us, people will forget what we do, but never how we make them feel.

Charles Dickens wrote that no one is useless in the world if they lighten the burdens of other people.

Where will I find significance?

What will make me feel that my contribution is significant to God, to my family, to others, to myself?

Fortunately God does not command me to be significant.

He simply commands me to love and trust in Him and show up to do what He gives me to do. He takes care of the significance.

- -

The will of God is not wrapped up in the details of what we do, but the character of who we are.
~ Randy Alcorn[lvii]

- - - - - - - - - - - - - - - - - - - -

Psalm 138:3
As soon as I pray, You answer me;
You encourage me by giving me strength.

- - - - - - - - - - - - - - - - - - - -

We are a community of people on an Accidental Sabbatical and we have the opportunity to be significant in someone else's life by helping each other. We can pray for each other at the very least.

Several people have helped me to meet recruiters, to rewrite my resume for the umpteenth time, to help me acclimate in this move and find my way around this new city.

Anyone who is creating a resume and writing a cover letter can use a second set of eyes (or more) to help them write it or read it or proofread it.

Do you know someone who has an interview scheduled and needs help with role-playing those behavioral questions?

Everyone you meet needs something, even as simple as a cup of coffee and a listening ear. Ask how you can help. Ask how you can pray. You will find that in helping others, you are the one being helped.

- -

Three billion people on the face of the earth go to bed hungry every night, but four billion people go to bed every night hungry for a simple word of encouragement and recognition.
~ Cavett Robert[lviii]

- -

Everyone needs someone to listen to them and to feel heard. Let them speak, unjudged. Let them whine or cry. Then encourage, validate and recognize their worth.

- -

Daniel 10:19
Don't be afraid, he said, for you are very precious to God. Peace! Be encouraged! Be strong!

- - - - - - - - - - - - - - - - - - -

When you are out networking and meeting people at various functions and events, are you only targeting people who can help you find a job? I have met several people doing just that… you know the ones who are talking with you, but mostly look over your head to see if there is someone else more important for them to approach. Similar to what I have seen on the red carpet on award shows… someone always looking for the more important person.

Wherever we go, we can find someone that we can help, whether or not they can do anything for us.

- - - - - - - - - - - - - - - - - -

You can have everything in life you want if you will just help enough other people get what they want.
~ Zig Ziglar[lix]

- - - - - - - - - - - - - - - - - -

Personal challenge:

What makes you feel significant? What has been your greatest accomplishment during this Accidental Sabbatical?

What can you do today to help someone else feel significant?

- -

- -

- -

***

Chapter 13: Doing

What we are *becoming* is because of what we are *doing*.

If we are hopeful, we are practicing hope.

If we simply stay busy but don't think about why we are doing things, too quickly meaningless activity will be filling up these precious open days. And then what will we become?

I have previously mentioned some of the ideas coming up here; the repetition is intentional.

- -

> *Setting goals is the first step in turning the invisible into the visible.* ~ *Tony Robbins*[lx]

- -

I have written down my annual goals for many years now. It is drilled into my head – if it isn't written down, it will not happen. So I write the goals down. Have you ever been given stretch goals at work? Now you are the boss of you, in your 'company of one', and you can come up with your own stretch goals and push yourself to reach them.

J.C. Penney is quoted as saying, Long-range goals keep you from being frustrated by short-term failures.

A year may not be considered 'long-range' to some people, but it really is. Especially when we are living day to day. I have learned that it is more than just writing down the goals though. I have to actually look at the list.

Every day.

– – – – – – – – – – – – – – – – – – –

Everything you will do in this year will come from what you do every day. Your year is made up of days.
~ Chris Brogan

– – – – – – – – – – – – – – – – – – –

Chris Brogan is CEO and publisher of Owner Media Group and author of several books. This statement of his has made a huge impact on me this year. It has helped me see each and every day as an important piece of the puzzle.

I have to look for job postings and talk to people if I hope to find a job. I need to write words every day to create a book. If I am to consult, I have to find the clients who need my help. I must do something *intentional* every day toward each of these goals.

– – – – – – – – – – – – – – – – – – –

Most of what we do on a daily basis won't matter in five minutes, much less five years. We do a lot that really doesn't matter. ~ Rick Warren

– – – – – – – – – – – – – – – – – – –

If I am not serious and intentional with my goals, I will walk away the first time it gets difficult. I know. I have done it before.

Write the goals down. Then break them down into steps. I track my goals using a spreadsheet. Ok, so it might sound a bit OCD, but spreadsheets work for me for tracking and organizing any kind of data. Use whatever process works for you. I create a spreadsheet for all my goals by January 1, prioritizing each goal with a due date.

The columns include:

GOAL

Action plan

Target date

Complete date

That's it. Intentionally simple.

For example, if my goal is to read 36 books this year, my action plan simply says read three books per month. If my goal is to become more healthy (fairly vague), the action item includes healthy eating and/or doing some exercise to make me sweat every day.

It's a list that I review every day, and update. I keep a list of the books I read, and a record of the progress toward becoming more healthy. I have additional goals on my list with even more specific details and steps outlined, but that gives you an idea of what the goal spreadsheet looks like and how simple it is to keep.

Every morning I open that spreadsheet and review my list. And that is the first important part of the exercise. There are great goals on the list but if I don't take any action toward them, they are wishes, not goals.

I push to read at least a book a week...so far so good. I am working on finishing a new book this year that I have been writing. I hope to get it done before my target date, as I know that when I become employed I won't have as much time to write.

Another goal is to be more healthy. I am not specifying an exact amount of pounds to lose; instead I am primarily working to break the sugar habit which is the best catalyst to reduce pounds. I also know I need to sweat every day to make progress. If I make choices with that goal in mind, my actions will move me toward success.

I also will increase my revenue this year. How? I have some ideas, but nothing firm yet. So on the goals list, I don't specify where the revenue will come from, just that it will be an increase over last year.

Do you have goals and have you written them down?

I am sure you have heard of S.M.A.R.T. goals: Specific. Measurable. Attainable. Relevant. Time-based. Or we could also call them H.A.R.D. goals: Heartfelt. Animated. Required. Difficult. No matter what words you plug in or what acrostic you create, most of us still need a plan to implement.

Are your goals broken down into manageable steps? Baby steps will be needed in some cases.

For example, I know that being healthier means I need to get more exercise, which takes time and pacing. I cannot instantly start running marathons. I started with parking my car in the back of the parking lot so that I have to walk. Then walking a bit farther – maybe a mile or two in the morning, and then before too long, I might be jogging.

I can start with a beginner yoga workout and work up to one of Bryan Kest's Power Yoga workouts. Or, there is always Jillian Michael's body-crusher-type workouts. Or Insanity with Shaun T., or P90X. There are many different ways to sweat every day. Start and work up to more intense options in due time.

- - - - - - - - - - - - - - - - - - - -

Philippians 3:14 (MSG)
I'm not saying that I have this all together, that I have it made. But I am well on my way, reaching out for Christ, who has so wondrously reached out for me. Friends, don't get me wrong: By no means do I count myself an expert in all of this, but I've got my eye on the goal, where God is beckoning us onward – to Jesus. I'm off and running, and I'm not turning back.

- - - - - - - - - - - - - - - - - - - -

It is the intentional action toward completing a goal that makes the difference. Intent plus action provides a sense of purpose and accomplishment during this Accidental Sabbatical.

- - - - - - - - - - - - - - - - - - - -

People who say that life is not worthwhile are really saying that they themselves have no personal goals

which are worthwhile... Get yourself a goal worth working for. Better still, get yourself a project... Always have something ahead of you to 'look forward to' - work for and hope for.
~ Maxwell Maltz[lxi]

— — — — — — — — — — — — — — — — — — — —

One thing I have always loved about doing project work is that by definition a project has a beginning, middle and end. The beginning always excites me... conceiving, planning, plotting, and then implementing. Depending on the type of project and its duration, the middle part of it is typically the most difficult. Then excitement returns as the project nears completion... a full circle... the end.

Whenever I need to get moving toward a goal, or just to get moving, I look for a project to do or I create one for myself. I have several projects lined up at this point.

Here are just a few on my personal project list that will take me days and maybe weeks to complete:

* Get the storage boxes out of the closet, scan all documents and then have a bonfire with the paper.

* Take the bin of photos that we have gathered over all these years and scan them into digital copies.

* Go through all clothes at least once every quarter and donate.

* Sell something online – eBay or Amazon, or Craigslist or somewhere. Take the photos, write the copy, try it!

I am pretty sure that if I actually get a regular nine to five job again that I will never get everything done.

What else is there to *do*?

Find new ways to be *living* life instead of just surviving life. Experiment. Try something new.

This is, after all, a sabbatical. Use the time to grow!

- -

Proverbs 18:15:
Intelligent people are always ready to learn. Their ears are open for knowledge.

- -

Take classes! Learn something new! Or take a refresher course on something you learned years ago. As I have mentioned before, Massive Open Online Courses – known as MOOC's - are available online at no charge, through several different websites. I have taken several courses at Coursera.org; I am in the middle of one on leadership right now.

Other options available may include classes at a local college. In our town, a community college has several classes offered at no charge if you are unemployed, designed to a) teach new skills, b) provide an opportunity to meet people and network and c) help in the career transition during your Accidental Sabbatical.

Then there are certifications to study and test on. One friend completed a class for certification in Data Analytics. He and several others in the networking groups have obtained their Project Management Professional (PMP) certification during their sabbatical.

Nurture yourself by nurturing others.

Volunteer your time at a local organization. Stuff envelopes for a non-profit doing a mailing. Help for a day or for a project, however long you like.

Once you make yourself available, the opportunities to help will find you.

Again, with this time available to us, we have all kinds of opportunity to learn new things, meet new people, start or finish projects we have wanted to do for years.

Are you taking advantage of the time?

* * *

Here are some quotes and scriptures I have in my Hope Box that speak to me about the importance of what I am doing during this time. I am not just treading water. I am doing important things. I have goals that have deadlines. I am thriving.

Zig Ziglar is one of my favorite motivational speakers. Just listening to him speak makes me smile! Of course you can find his videos on YouTube.

- - - - - - - - - - - - - - - - - - -

When obstacles arise, you change your direction to reach your goal, you do not change your decision to get there.
~ Zig Ziglar[lxii]

- - - - - - - - - - - - - - - - - -

Search 'motivational speaking' on YouTube; more than two million results popping up. If my mind is full of positive motivation, and I have goals and projects, I will have no time for worry and stress.

- - - - - - - - - - - - - - - - -

Vision is not enough. It must be combined with Venture. It is not enough to stare up the steps, we must step up the stairs.
~ Vaclav Havel[lxiii]

- - - - - - - - - - - - - - - - -

So what are you doing today that is worth a day of your life?

* * *

Personal challenge:
Brainstorm! Write a list of goals for yourself.
Create a spreadsheet if that works for you.
Write down your primary goal – the most important one.

- - - - - - - - - - - - - - - - - - -

- - - - - - - - - - - - - - - - - - -

- - - - - - - - - - - - - - - - - - -

- - - - - - - - - - - - - - - - - - -

- - - - - - - - - - - - - - - - - - -

What steps are you taking today to meet your most important goal?

- -

- -

- -

- -

- -

- -

* * *

Chapter 14: Resources

It is never too late to be something new or to be a better version of you. Find resources and begin with hope.

It would be nice if there were specific instructions that, if followed perfectly would guarantee employment. Unfortunately I have not found those magic procedures or I would have already written a procedure manual. Job hunting is not an exact science. There are few absolutes and no formula. So, in the absence of a formula and exact procedures, here are some ideas and resources that have been helpful to me and to others in my Accidental Sabbatical. I share them hoping that you will benefit from them as well.

By far my greatest resource has been prayer... my own prayers, and those of others who believe in God's power and who pray for me.

- -

Nehemiah 1:11
O Lord, please hear my prayer! Listen to the prayers
of those of us who delight in honoring you. Please

*grant me success today by making the king favorable
to me. Put it into his heart to be kind to me.*

– – – – – – – – – – – – – – – – – –

Praying releases me to be calm and confident that God has my circumstances in sight and in His hands.

With prayer comes faith, and with faith comes action.

Some of the following ideas have helped me to *be*... To be happy with myself, content in this situation and to maintain my health and sanity.

These are also ideas listed here for things to *do*. Ideas for training and transition, personal growth and other networking ideas.

Finally, here are some places to *belong*. Groups to join. Places to volunteer skills or service.

I am sure you can add to the list. There is a place to do so at the end of the chapter and then I created a blog where we all can continue to share ideas and resources. If you will join me, please share your ideas here:

http://accidentalsabbatical.wordpress.com/

So, here are some of my resources; things to do for positive change, sanity and personal growth:

Focus on your health both physical and mental.

Yoga: If you don't have a DVD or CD for yoga, you can find it on YouTube – there are multiple levels from beginner to advanced. Just search 'yoga' and choose your level. I am currently doing a 30 Day Yoga Challenge.

Then there is Jillian Michaels' 30 Day Shred: Level 1:

http://www.youtube.com/watch?v=1Pc-NizMgg8

She has several of her level 1 videos from her various workout plans posted on YouTube, so choose the one that works for your fitness level, and get started. Or if her style doesn't work for you, search for workouts with another fitness leader.

Join a gym! There are many options in many price brackets.

I read about someone who was living out of his car, who kept a cheap gym membership to stay in shape and also to have a place available 24-hours a day to take a shower.

Eat healthfully!

IncredibleSmoothies! This is Tracy and Davy Russell's website with nutritional information and recipes for green smoothies:

http://www.incrediblesmoothies.com/category/recipes/

This Pineapple-Broccoli Smoothie is one of my favorites:

http://www.incrediblesmoothies.com/recipes/broccoli-pineapple-green-smoothie-recipe/

When I started drinking green smoothies for breakfast last year, I began by following her recipes exactly until I created my own combination of greens and fruit that tastes good and is cost effective. I subscribe to her emails and receive new recipe ideas to alleviate boredom from using the same recipe all the time. And her site is just one of many that offer smoothie recipes online.

Another online resource for health and nutrition ideas is this Calorie Count site that allows us to log food intake and activity and provides feedback of nutrient specifics.

http://caloriecount.about.com/

Another site I recently discovered is CRON-O-Meter, that provides a comprehensive nutrition analysis:

https://cronometer.com/

If you struggle with what I call "eating awareness", as I often do, these sites help me to be aware of how many calories I consume, and the resulting nutritional impact, which is a tremendous catalyst to working on my goal. Just logging everything I eat causes me to think twice if I know I have to report it.

There are many other health and wellness options to explore, and now that we have the time to take care of our bodies, we have eliminated the first big excuse. At least I have.

Learn something new!

Massive Open Online Courses (MOOC's) are free online college courses available at hundreds of global universities. https://Redhoop.com is a site that aggregates information on courses from several different sources. Find MOOC's here:

Coursera: https://www.coursera.org/
edX: https://www.edx.org/
Udacity: https://www.udacity.com/
Khan Academy: http://www.khanacademy.org/

Choose an area of interest, you will definitely find something to study on at least one of these sites.

Free. Yes, these courses are free. Some of them offer additional 'verified' certificates for a nominal fee, but there is much to learn at no charge.

I have taken several courses at Coursera.org, originally started with 33 elite universities, now with more than 600 global partners.

Another option is a site featuring leading UK and international universities:

https://www.futurelearn.com/

There may even be other new sites by the time you get this in your hands, so search online for "MOOC" and see what you can find. I just did and there were millions of results.

Not only do we have the advantage of a free education in these online courses but in addition there is a Discussion Forum in each class where you can communicate with thousands of other students from all over the world. So it provides a networking avenue unlike any other.

There are other ways to learn something new without committing to taking an entire class. TED Talks are "Ideas worth spreading" on Technology, Entertainment and Design and are another great resource and "clearinghouse of free knowledge from the world's most inspired thinkers", as described on their About page.

The videos range from 10 to 20 minutes long, given by experts in a field, with the intention to spread ideas and spark conversation. Find one (or ten) that interests you here:

http://www.ted.com/ or on YouTube, or TED TV programs or radio hours. There are many ways to 'get TED'.

I have spent hours absorbing information on this site and I could share several of them. But here are just two of my favorites. Both of these TED speakers have written books that are on my book list in chapter three.

— — — — — — — — — — — — — — — — — — —

Shawn Achor at TEDx Bloomington in May 2011:
"The Happy Secret to Better Work":
http://www.ted.com/talks/shawn_achor_the_happy_s
ecret_to_better_work

— — — — — — — — — — — — — — — — — — —

Brené Brown at TED2012 in March 2012:
Listening to Shame:
*http://www.ted.com/talks/brene_brown_listening_to_*
shame

— — — — — — — — — — — — — — — — — — —

Additionally, several of the professors in Coursera have been TED speakers. When I am debating on taking a class and need to know how the professor delivers information, I often search to see if they have done a TED talk and listen. Dan Ariely with Duke University is my favorite. Search for his talks on behavior.

Remember what Jim Rohn said about becoming the average of the five people you hang out with most often? If you need to find brilliant positive people, add TED speakers to your daily schedule.

Read and Listen

In addition to the books I listed in a previous chapter, there is so much to read online. Online magazines and blogs in all areas of entrepreneurship, business, leadership, writing, and, of course, our ongoing current need for advice the job search.

Among others, I read these blogs:

Seth Godin: http://sethgodin.typepad.com/

Mark Schaefer's 'Grow':

http://www.businessesgrow.com/

Ownermag.com is a digital magazine written by Chris Brogan that provides insight, instruction and inspiration for business owners: http://ownermag.com/.

There are blogtalk radio shows that offer advice on any number of subjects. Pick a podcast that interests you: http://www.blogtalkradio.com/

There are daily TED Talks that arrive in my inbox.

I repeat - what I let into my mind has a huge impact on my day and every element of this journey so I am very selective.

These are sites that I visit regularly; some of which provide networking opportunities so critical to the job search:

Specifically On Careers:

LinkedIn: https://www.linkedin.com/nhome/

I am going to assume that if you haven't just crawled out from under a rock in the past five or so years, you are aware of LinkedIn and its importance in your job search. Figure out what works best for you as you will find a multitude of opinions on the "correct" way to create your profile, share your experience, both on LinkedIn and your resume. I have found that for every expert telling me one thing, a different 'expert' will tell me to do the exact opposite. While there are a few common denominators, take the best from each advisor when you create your own.

After all you are portraying yourself to the world, and you must feel comfortable and confident with what you say about yourself and how you say it, especially online.

Careerealism: Because Every Job is Temporary

Careerealism is an online career advice and job search site with outstanding career experts helping people solve career and job search problems. J.T. O'Donnell founded this organization and she provides webinars and has archives of amazing advice!

http://www.careerealism.com/

Be very picky about who you let influence your brain!

Services You May Need

I have tried to stay focused on areas I can speak of personally, however one friend suggested I include information on health insurance and personal counselors or coaches. So some of these next ideas have come from friends' recommendations or online research.

Health insurance options:

1. Continuation of Health Coverage - COBRA: In the United States, the Consolidated Omnibus Budget Reconciliation Act (COBRA) requires that an employer with 20 or more employees, offer their employees and their families the opportunity to temporarily extend their health insurance coverage for 18 months. Typically the cost is significantly higher than you were paying as an employee, nevertheless it is an option. If you are unaware of this provision, the Department of Labor's website has more information:

http://www.dol.gov/dol/topic/health-plans/cobra.htm

2. As of this publication date in 2014, in the United States, the Affordable Care Act is a new law that provides a vehicle for all Americans to purchase health insurance. Information on the options and the Health Insurance Marketplace may be found on this federal government website: https://www.healthcare.gov/

The options also differ by state, so search online for what might be available in your state.

3. Private temporary insurance: There are short term health plans available to individuals and families that provide for the 'gap' between long-term health plans. Search for "short term or temporary health insurance between jobs" and there are several options available.

In the past, as students we purchased this type of gap insurance also known as 'catastrophic health plans'. It had a $10,000 deductible and very limited coverage, however it was affordable and provided peace of mind.

* * *

There are also Career transition coaches or personal counselors. In addition to career resources available in the form of articles and webinars, you may want to talk with someone face to face.

There are coaches everywhere it seems, so I would investigate anyone who approaches you to offer their coaching services to make sure they are in fact certified or legitimate. If your resume is on LinkedIn or other job boards, your email address is available to anyone, so be careful.

I have met a few job seekers who have benefited from the services of career transition counselors, some even receiving this career coaching as part of their layoff package. There are other firms that make these services available directly to individuals who hire them. I personally have not located any that are free. However search online for career transition services in your local area and see what you find.

There are also career coaches, life coaches, business coaches, you name it, there's a coach. If you choose to work with one, look for a certified coach. The two non-profit coach certification organizations that are most recognized are these:

International Association of Coaching (IAC): http://www.certifiedcoach.org/
International Coach Federation (ICF): http://coachfederation.org/

Some coaches offer advice and ideas online, whether on their own website or social media, often giving something free to show what they have to offer, to build relationships so you will hire them. Pamela Slim, mentioned earlier, is the author of two books I recommend, and she also is a career coach. http://pamelaslim.com/

Pam Slim did provide a free call once a month where she generously took questions and gave advice on careers and small businesses. I have been on many of those calls and have often been surprised at her willingness to share so much of her knowledge and experience at no charge. In doing so, she definitely earned my trust and I have bought and read her books.

Another job seeker told me about a certified life coach in my area whose focus is on life balance and personal growth, both critical factors in career transition.

Personal counseling can be another valuable resource during the Accidental Sabbatical. One friend told me that some companies offer their employees and their spouses free counseling sessions through difficult or transitional life situations. She shared with me that her counselor listened to her concerns, gave her tools to help diffuse anxiety and offered sound advice and encouragement. She described the counselor as "Jesus with skin on" who helped her keep her sanity.

I have not pursued counseling for myself, because I have a very strong support system in my husband and my family so it frankly has never occurred to me to do so. However, if I were going to, I would first pray that the Lord would lead me to find a good one. Then I would check to see if it would be covered through health insurance and find a provider there. Then next, as I do when searching for any service, I would ask friends and family for referrals and then search online for information and reviews on those recommended professionals.

(NOTE: when I say 'search online' I may 'Google' the information, however I also use other search engines such as Bing or DuckDuckgo.com, that does not track a search.)

Find a group to join!

Join Meetups to find job seeker groups, or other groups that share your interests.

http://www.meetup.com/

You can also create your own group and invite others to join.

Find a good cause where you can volunteer your time: http://www.volunteermatch.org/

If you sing or play an instrument, find a church looking for choir or orchestra members. Additionally, there are often many kinds of small groups within a church that you can join. Typically the larger the church, the more small groups you will find within them. That is how they build community within a large church.

Find a small group to join somewhere. Anywhere.

Join a group of runners, or a book club, or a group that meets regularly for coffee or lunch. I attend networking luncheons with the Connected Women of NC to meet people in my new town. In addition to good career contacts, the unexpected blessing has been that a couple of real friendships have resulted.

I have also just joined a coffee and book club meetup, two of my favorite things.

To find other networking ideas a quick search on the Meetup site for "networking" within 50 miles of my home results in 1754 meetups nearby. I guarantee that you can find at least one small group to join.

* * *

Personal Challenge:

What resources can you add to this list?

What group are you going to join?

What could you do today to be a resource for someone else?

\- \-

\- \-

\- \-

\- \-

\- \-

\- \-

\- \-

\- \-

\- \-

\- \-

* * *

*NOTE: All of the above links were active hyperlinks as of the publication date of this book. At the time of this writing, none of these links are currently affiliate links, however the following disclosure is required on blog websites so I am including the disclosure here:

"Disclosure of Material Connection: Some of the links in the post above may be "affiliate links". This means if you click on the link and purchase the item, I may receive an affiliate commission. I only recommend products or services I use personally and believe will add value to my readers. I am disclosing this in accordance with the Federal Trade Commission's 16 CFR, Part 255: "Guides Concerning the Use of Endorsements and Testimonials in Advertising."

* * *

Chapter 15: Celebrate!

— — — — — — — — — — — — — — — — — —

Psalm 150: 1-2

Praise the Lord! Praise God in His sanctuary; praise Him in His mighty heaven! Praise Him for His mighty works; praise His unequaled greatness!

— — — — — — — — — — — — — — — — — —

Let's celebrate hope!!

If it is time to celebrate your new job, I will celebrate that with you. We will all celebrate the job when we begin that new season! However, let's also celebrate the Accidental Sabbatical and the gift that it is!

Trust that there is a reason for your Accidental Sabbatical.

Wherever we are right now, let's be there. Let's enjoy it. Celebrate it. We may not be where we thought we would be by now, but we are getting there. I am enjoying what may seem like little things now; someday I will know if they were big things.

Emily Freeman wrote on this subject in her blog, *Chatting at the Sky*, reminding us that it is a temptation to be looking to what will be coming, whatever the next big thing is going to be, and idealizing not only what was, but what we think will be in the future. Instead we need to embrace what is now.

I praise the Lord for his gift of calm and peace during this season. For me this Accidental Sabbatical has been a time of reflection, learning, growth, healing, faith-building, goal-reaching, to name just a few of the blessings. It has had purpose.

If I started a new job tomorrow, could I look back on these months and find purpose in what I did? Would I celebrate how I have lived and was I faithful with what I was given to do? I believe so.

- - - - - - - - - - - - - - - - - - - -

Matthew 25:23
Well done, my good and faithful servant. You have been faithful in handling this small amount, so now I will give you many more responsibilities.
Let's celebrate together!

- - - - - - - - - - - - - - - - - - - -

Others have shared with me how their Accidental Sabbaticals have provided gifts in their lives.

One gentleman spent years on the road as a high level salesperson. He shared with me that his layoff provided him with six months at home with his family, giving him time to get to know his wife and teenage kids again. He celebrated when he found new employment, and most of all he celebrates that he is forever changed by his Accidental Sabbatical season.

A single mother's teenage son developed a medical condition that took months to correctly diagnose and treat. God knew that she would need the time and all of her attention to work on this much more important mission. Fortunately they found answers and during those months that her son was healing, she found consulting contracts that enabled her to not only support them during that time but to successfully launch her own consulting business.

Another woman had wanted to move back to her home state to be near her aging parents. But her job had not allowed that to happen... until her department was eliminated and she was laid off. Her job search then expanded to her home state and she told me she would know if it was the right time to move back if she found employment there rather than here. And she did, so she moved.

Another friend recently moved to Florida to start a new contract job! After more than a year without work and draining all of her savings, she is once again earning money! It is not 'regular employment' and it might not last, but it's a gift and hope for today.

Even after getting a job, some people are expressing valid concerns about whether they will be able to keep the job or whether they can even still do it... did they lose their skills... are they still able to deal with the stress...

Doubts can creep in and threaten to wipe out joy. And that is yet another reason to celebrate! Keep the enemy of doubt away by praising the Lord.

This is another verse from my Hope Box that I read frequently. Especially during those times that my stomach knots when I worry that I might even get a job and fail. As long as I remember that he is with me no matter what, I can be strong and have no doubt.

- -

Joshua 1:9
This is my command – be strong and courageous! Do not be afraid or discouraged. For the Lord your God is with you wherever you go.

- -

God promises to restore, support and strengthen us.

- -

1 Peter 5:10
In His kindness God called you to share in His eternal glory by means of Christ Jesus. So after you have suffered a little while, He will restore, support, and strengthen you, and He will place you on a firm foundation.

- -

Many of us are still waiting for a new job. While I wait I celebrate the surprises of hope that he gives me.

I can be surprised by hope when a great phone interview leads to an onsite interview, which may lead me to my next assignment. I celebrate each new possibility and the new hope that it gives me.

We are learning to be patient in these circumstances, finding new places to belong, and doing new things with our lives, right? I don't believe God is punishing us or intentionally inflicting suffering. He is using our circumstances to strengthen us and bring us closer to him, especially if we let him.

He has given me this gift of time to spend with him and to be alert for his surprises.

- -

Each day holds a surprise. But only if we expect it can we see, hear, or feel it when it comes to us. Let's not be afraid to receive each day's surprise, whether it comes to us as sorrow or as joy. It will open a new place in our hearts, a place where we can welcome new friends and celebrate more fully our shared humanity.

~ Henri Nouwen[lxiv]

- -

Will we land our career dream positions? Will we get them back? Maybe. Maybe not. Time will tell. Perhaps we will have a new dream and go in a totally different direction now that leads us to more joy in our work than ever before.

Is the sabbatical really accidental?

I believe my Accidental Sabbatical is actually the next assignment God had waiting for me. As with many other projects I have done, it has been long and challenging, and I pray I have remained faithful on the journey.

Although a different season that includes a 'regular job' is not yet in sight, I am thriving now and although this may be the end of this book, I can celebrate hope because the end of the story is *To Be Continued...*

THE END

About the Author

Shari Risoff spent years communicating in the corporate world in addition to writing newsletters and appeal letters for non-profit organizations. She became an author of books during her Accidental Sabbatical.

Her first book, _Released: A True Story of Escape from an Abusive Marriage_ is a personal memoir about how she was freed from an abusive marriage and released to begin a new life.

She lives in North Carolina with her husband Stephen. When she is not writing, she is observing, or reading or studying human behavior. Or, more importantly, she is hanging out with Stephen, the love of her life and soul mate.

Her goal in everything she writes is to share God's love and His grace in her life in the words.

Notes and Additional Resources

The scripture verses included in this text are taken from the New Living Translation version of the Holy Bible, unless other another version is noted. The entire Bible is available online, and the source I use is Bible Gateway: http://www.biblegateway.com/

Additionally, throughout the book, several resources are cited and a source is identified in the Endnotes section. Here are some additional resources for further reading and interaction:

Chapter 1

J.T. O'Donnell, Careerealism.com webinar: *Got FIRED: How to Explain it to Potential Employers* (9/17/2013) http://www.careerealism.com/got-fired-how-to-explain-to-potential-employers/#!QF7R2

Lamott, Anne, *Bird by Bird.* (New York: Anchor Books, a division of Random House), 1995.
More about Anne Lamott, as well as a list of all of her books can be found on her Amazon author's page: http://amzn.to/1odsJ2r

Lucado, Max, *God Came Near.* (Nashville: Thomas Nelson), 2004.
More about Max Lucado, as well as a list of all of his books can be found on his Amazon author's page: http://amzn.to/1kx9tK8

Chapter 2
Os Hillman. For additional resources or to subscribe to TGIF, Today God is First devotionals go to http://www.marketplaceleaders.org/tgif/

Pastor Rick Warren of Saddleback Church in California, http://saddleback.com/ connects and shares in social media, on Twitter (@RickWarren), on his Facebook page and LinkedIn Group:
Facebook: https://www.facebook.com/pastorrickwarren
LinkedIn Group: "Pastor Rick Warren"
More about Rick Warren, as well as a list of all of his books can be found on his Amazon author's page: http://amzn.to/1gpLAog

Vujicic, Nick, *Life Without Limits.* (Colorado Springs: WaterBrook Press, Reprint edition), 2012.
More about Nick Vujicic, as well as a list of all of his books can be found on his Amazon author's page: http://amzn.to/1tukOgI

Chapter 3
Corrie Ten Boom wrote several books: *The Hiding Place,* 1971, 1984 & 2006; *Amazing Love: True Stories of the Power of Forgiveness,* 2007. *In My Father's House,* 2011... to name just a few. You will find a complete list here in her bookshop: http://www.corrietenboom.com/bookshop2.htm

Chapter 4

Maxwell, John C., *21 Irrefutable Laws of Leadership,* (Nashville: Thomas Nelson) 2007. The PLAN AHEAD acrostic is found in the Law of Navigation, page 43.

More about John C. Maxwell, as well as a list of all of his books can be found on his Amazon author's page: http://amzn.to/1nB5xat

Chapter 5

Joni Eareckson Tada is the founder and CEO of Joni and Friends International Disability Center. More information, including her books and other resources available on their website: http://www.joniandfriends.org/

Jim Rohn's books, and other resources may be found on his website: http://www.jimrohn.com/resource-library.html

Bernstein, Albert & Rozen, Sydney Craft, *Neanderthals at Work: How People and Politics Can Drive You Crazy…And What You Can Do About Them,* (New York: Balantine Books) 1996; (originally published 1992 by John Wiley, now out of print).

Kay Arthur is a Bible teacher and the cofounder of Precept Ministries International. More information and resources are available on their site: http://precept.org/home

Billy Graham is an American Christian evangelist, who has ministered all over the world for 60 years. More information and resources are available on the Billy Graham Association website: http://billygraham.org/

Chapter 6
Wilkerson, Mike, *Redemption: Freed by Jesus from the Idols We Worship and the Wounds We Carry*. (Wheaton: Crossway Books), 2011.
More about Mike Wilkerson, as well as a list of all of his books can be found on his Amazon author's page: http://amzn.to/TCR2KD

Richard Bach is a writer. Additional information on Richard Bach may be found on his website: http://richardbach.com/

Dr. Henry Blackaby wrote the original *Experiencing God: Knowing and Doing the Will of God*, (Nashville: Lifeway Press) in 1991. Updated versions, additional information and more resources of Dr. Blackaby's and the Blackaby Ministries International may be found on the website: http://www.blackaby.net/store/

Lubbock, John. *The Use of Life*. Originally published by London: MacMillan & Co. 1894.

Chan, Francis, *Crazy Love: Overwhelmed by a Relentless God*, (Colorado Springs: David C. Cook), 2013.
More about Francis Chan, as well as a list of his books may be found on his Amazon author's page: http://amzn.to/1lIRP2L

Chapter 7
W. Edwards Deming. Considered the 'father of quality', Dr. Deming is an international consultant in quality and productivity management. More about Dr. Deming, as well as a list of his books may be found on the site of The W. Edwards Deming Institute: https://www.deming.org/

Chapter 8
Simon Sinek. Inspirational writer and speaker on leadership. One of my favorite TED Talk speakers. More information on his books and work on his site: https://www.startwithwhy.com/

Chapter 9
Watchman Nee. A Christian minister and writer in mainland China, imprisoned for his faith from 1952 until he died in prison in 1972. More information can be found on his website: http://www.watchmannee.org/ and a list of his books may be found on his Amazon author page: http://amzn.to/1hhKFBn

Pete Wilson. Author and Pastor of Cross Point Church in Nashville, TN, http://www.crosspoint.tv/
More information about Pete Wilson as well as a list of his books may be found on his Amazon author page: http://amzn.to/1hkQgH4

Davis, Justin and Davis, Trisha, *Beyond Ordinary: When a Good Marriage Just Isn't Good Enough.* (Wheaton: Tyndale House Publishers), 2012.

Chapter 10
Lotz, Anne Graham. *The Vision of His Glory.* (Nashville: Thomas Nelson), 1997.
More about Anne Graham Lotz, as well as a list of all of her books may be found on her Amazon author's page: http://amzn.to/1kbwv9C

Al Jarreau. One of my favorite jazz artists. Find his work at his Amazon Artist store: http://amzn.to/1nBlQEj

Chapter 11
Henri Nouwen. Information is available at this website on Henri Nouwen's books and other resources: http://www.henrinouwen.org/

Chapter 12
Adrian Rogers. More about Adrian Rogers and a list of his books can be found on his Amazon author's page: http://amzn.to/1ic6J0h and on the Love Worth Finding Ministries website: http://www.lwf.org/site/PageNavigator/about/adrian_rogers

Kushner, Harold (Rabbi). *When All You've Ever Wanted Isn't Enough: The Search for a Life That Matters.* (New York: Simon & Schuster Inc.), 2002.

Randy Alcorn. Author and founder of Eternal Perspective Ministries, His books are all available on their website: http://www.epm.org/books/

Zig Ziglar. All of Zig Ziglar's books and personal development products may be found on his website: http://www.ziglar.com/

Chapter 13
Anthony Robbins. More information about Anthony Robbins and his leadership and motivational books and resources may be found on his website: http://www.anthonyrobbins.com/

Chris Brogan. More information about Chris Brogan's books, coaching and other resources may be found on his websites: http://www.chrisbrogan.com/; http://ownermag.com/ and http://www.humanbusinessworks.com/

Chapter 14
Pamela Slim. More information on Pam Slim's books and coaching may be found on her website: http://pamelaslim.com/

Chapter 15
Henri Nouwen. A list of Henri Nouwen's books may be found on his Amazon author's page. http://amzn.to/TH6eWV

*NOTE: All of the above links were active hyperlinks as of the publication date of this book. At the time of this publication, none of these links are currently affiliate links; however the following disclosure is required on blog websites so I am including it here:

"Disclosure of Material Connection: Some of the links in the post above may be "affiliate links". This means if you click on the link and purchase the item, I may receive an affiliate commission. I only recommend products or services I use personally and believe will add value to my readers. I am disclosing this in accordance with the Federal Trade Commission's 16 CFR, Part 255: "Guides Concerning the Use of Endorsements and Testimonials in Advertising."

Endnotes

* Some of the quotes in this book are referenced in multiple locations; these endnotes provide one source.

i Anne Lamott. (1994). *Bird by Bird*.

ii Max Lucado. (n.d.) Maxlucado.com. Retrieved 12 March 2014 from http://maxlucado.com/audio/daily-audio/unpredictable-dependence/

iii C.S. Lewis. (2002) *Letters to Malcolm: Chiefly on Prayer*. Retrieved 28 April 2014 from https://www.goodreads.com/quotes/81972-relying-on-god-has-to-begin-all-over-again-every

iv Blaise Pascal. (n.d.). BrainyQuote.com. Retrieved 09 May 2014, from BrainyQuote.com:
http://www.brainyquote.com/quotes/quotes/b/blaisepasc390555.html

v Philip Yancey. (n.d.) Goodreads.com. Retrieved 08 May 2014 from https://www.goodreads.com/quotes/195520-i-have-learned-that-faith-means-trusting-in-advance-what

vi Timothy Willard. (19 February 2014). Into Great Silence. Retrieved 12 March 2014 from http://www.timothywillard.com/blog/2014/2/19/into-great-silence

vii Aldous Huxley. (n.d.). BrainyQuote.com. Retrieved 08 March 2014, from BrainyQuote.com:
http://www.brainyquote.com/quotes/quotes/a/aldoushuxl145888.html

viii Os Hillman, Today God Is First daily inspiration:
http://www.marketplaceleaders.org/

ix Steve Jobs. (n.d.). BrainyQuote.com. Retrieved 08 March 2014, from BrainyQuote.com:
http://www.brainyquote.com/quotes/quotes/s/stevejobs416859.html

x Rick Warren. (05 February 2014). Retrieved 25 March 2014 from https://www.facebook.com/pastorrickwarren/posts/10152231043410903

xi Nick Vujicic. (2010) *Life Without Limits*.

xii J.R.R. Tolkien. (1967) *The Fellowship of the Ring*.

xiii Vernon Howard. (n.d.) Goodreads.com. Retrieved 08 April 2014 from http://www.goodreads.com/quotes/199428-do-not-be-impatient-with-your-seemingly-slow-progress-do xiv Earl of Chesterfield Philip D. Stanhope, Eugenia Stanhope, (1747) The Letters of the Earl of Chesterfield to His Son, Volume 1, Letter CXXXI.

xv Abraham Harold Maslow. (n.d.) Goodreads.com. Retrieved 17 March 2014 from http://www.goodreads.com/quotes/118145-one-can-choose-to-go-back-toward-safety-or-forward

xvi H. G. Wells. (n.d.). BrainyQuote.com. Retrieved 08 March 2014, from BrainyQuote.com:
http://www.brainyquote.com/quotes/quotes/h/hgwells121062.html

xvii Joseph Campbell. (n.d.). BrainyQuote.com. Retrieved 08 March 2014, from BrainyQuote.com:
http://www.brainyquote.com/quotes/quotes/j/josephcamp386014.html

xviii Jim Rohn. (n.d.). BrainyQuote.com. Retrieved 08 March 2014, from BrainyQuote.com:
http://www.brainyquote.com/quotes/quotes/j/jimrohn147499.html

xix Mike Murdock. (n.d.). BrainyQuote.com. Retrieved 08 March 2014, from BrainyQuote.com:
http://www.brainyquote.com/quotes/quotes/m/mikemurdoc185325.html

xx Anne Lamott, (2005). Plan B: Further Thoughts on Faith.

xxi Albert J. Bernstein, Sydney C. Rozen, (1992). Neanderthals at Work: How People and Politics Can Drive You Crazy…And What You Can Do About Them.

xxii Kay Arthur. (2010). When the Hurt Runs Deep: Healing and Hope for Life's Desperate Moments.

xxiii Dwight D. Eisenhower. (n.d.). BrainyQuote.com. Retrieved 29 April 2014, from BrainyQuote.com:
http://www.brainyquote.com/quotes/quotes/d/dwightdei107094.html

xxiv Helen Keller. (n.d.). BrainyQuote.com. Retrieved 29 April 2014, from BrainyQuote.com:
http://www.brainyquote.com/quotes/quotes/h/helenkelle121787.html

xxv Earl Nightingale. (n.d.). BrainyQuote.com. Retrieved 29 April 2014, from BrainyQuote.com:
http://www.brainyquote.com/quotes/quotes/e/earlnighti159037.html

xxvi Billy Graham. (n.d.). BrainyQuote.com. Retrieved 29 April 2014, from BrainyQuote.com:
http://www.brainyquote.com/quotes/quotes/b/billygraha384427.html

xxvii John C. Maxwell. (n.d.). BrainyQuote.com. Retrieved 29 April 2014, from BrainyQuote.com: http://www.brainyquote.com/quotes/quotes/j/johncmaxw600890.html

xxviii Mike Wilkerson. (2011). Redemption: Freed by Jesus from the Idols We Worship and the Wounds We Carry.

xxix Richard Bach. (n.d.). BrainyQuote.com. Retrieved 10 March 2014, from BrainyQuote.com: http://www.brainyquote.com/quotes/quotes/r/richardbac132675.html

xxx Dr. Henry Blackaby. (1990) *Experiencing God.*

xxxi Rumi. (n.d.) Goodreads.com. Retrieved 13 May 2014 from https://www.goodreads.com/quotes/475219-sorrow-prepares-you-for-joy-it-violently-sweeps-everything-out

xxxii John Lubbock. (n.d.). BrainyQuote.com. Retrieved 20 March 2014, from BrainyQuote.com: http://www.brainyquote.com/quotes/quotes/j/johnlubboc107976.html

xxxiii Francis Chan. (2013). Crazy Love: Overwhelmed by a Relentless God.

xxxiv W. Edwards Deming. (n.d.). BrainyQuote.com. Retrieved 10 March 2014, from BrainyQuote.com: http://www.brainyquote.com/quotes/quotes/w/wedwardsd163061.html

xxxv Robert Brault. (n.d.) Quoteswave.com Retrieved 10 March 2014 from http://www.quoteswave.com/picture-quotes/383361

xxxvi Frank McCourt. (n.d.). Goodreads.com. Retrieved 10 March 2014 from http://www.goodreads.com/author/quotes/3347.Frank_McCourt

xxxvii Earl Nightingale. (n.d.) Goodreads.com. Retrieved 21 March 2014 from http://www.goodreads.com/quotes/32384-never-give-up-on-a-dream-just-because-of-the

xxxviii Stephen King. (n.d.) Goodreads.com. Retrieved 21 March 2014 from http://www.goodreads.com/quotes/76668-talent-is-cheaper-than-table-salt-what-separates-the-talented

xxxix Booker T. Washington. (n.d.). BrainyQuote.com. Retrieved 21 March 2014, from BrainyQuote.com: http://www.brainyquote.com/quotes/quotes/b/bookertwa107996.html

xl Og Mandino. (n.d.) Goodreads.com Retrieved 21 March 2014 from http://www.goodreads.com/quotes/753992-i-will-persist-until-i-succeed-always-will-i-take

xli Jack Canfield. (n.d.) Goodreads.com. Retrieved 21 March 2014 from http://www.goodreads.com/quotes/29794-don-t-worry-about-failures-worry-about-the-chances-you-miss

xlii Abraham Lincoln. (n.d.). BrainyQuote.com. Retrieved 21 March 2014, from BrainyQuote.com: http://www.brainyquote.com/quotes/quotes/a/abrahamlin121354.html

xliii Watchman Nee quoted by Os Hillman in Marketplace Meditations. Retrieved 12 May 2014 from http://www.crosswalk.com/devotionals/marketplace/marketplace-meditations-2-or-10-546882.html

xliv Pete Wilson. (03 March 2014) You'll Reap What You Sow. Retrieved 10 March 2014 from http://www.withoutwax.tv/2014/03/03/youll-reap-what-you-sow/

xlv Napoleon Hill. (n.d.) Goodreads.com. Retrieved 21 March 2014 from http://www.goodreads.com/quotes/810607-remember-the-thoughts-that-you-think-and-the-statements-you

xlvi Donald Grey Barnhouse. (n.d.) Theranch.org. Retrieved 17 March 2014 from http://theranch.org/2013/07/29/donald-grey-barnhouse-i-can-say-from-experience/

xlvii Abraham Lincoln. (n.d.). BrainyQuote.com. Retrieved 21 March 2014, from BrainyQuote.com: http://www.brainyquote.com/quotes/quotes/a/abrahamlin121094.html

xlviii Marcus Tullius Cicero. (n.d.). BrainyQuote.com. Retrieved 21 March 2014, from BrainyQuote.com: http://www.brainyquote.com/quotes/quotes/m/marcustull122152.html

xlix Anne Graham Lotz. (1997). The Vision of His Glory, page 24.

l Al Jarreau. (n.d.). BrainyQuote.com. Retrieved 07 March 2014, from BrainyQuote.com: http://www.brainyquote.com/quotes/quotes/a/aljarreau264412.html

li Elbert Hubbard. (n.d.). Goodreads.com. Retrieved 10 March 2014 from https://www.goodreads.com/quotes/835131-there-is-only-one-way-to-avoid-criticism-do-nothing

[lii] Eleanor Roosevelt. (n.d.). Goodreads.com. Retrieved 07 March 2014, from http://www.goodreads.com/author/quotes/44566.Eleanor_Roosevelt

[liii] Henri J. M. Nouwen, (1996). Can You Drink the Cup? Page 56.

[liv] Mother Teresa. (n.d.). BrainyQuote.com. Retrieved 07 March 2014, from BrainyQuote.com: http://www.brainyquote.com/quotes/quotes/m/mothertere106501.html

[lv] Adrian Rogers. (13 March 2014). Christianity.com. Love Worth Finding. Retrieved 14 March 2014 from http://www.christianity.com/devotionals/love-worth-finding-adrian-rogers/love-worth-finding-march-13.html

[lvi] Harold S. Kushner. (2002) When All You've Ever Wanted Isn't Enough: The Search for a Life That Matters. Page 18.

[lvii] Randy Alcorn, Eternal Perspective Ministries, 39085 Pioneer Blvd., Suite 206, Sandy, OR 97055, www.epm.org

[lviii] Cavett Robert, quoted in Aldric, Marshall. (2009). *Success Behind the Scars*, page 164.

[lix] Zig Ziglar. (n.d.). BrainyQuote.com. Retrieved 02 May 2014, from BrainyQuote.com: http://www.brainyquote.com/quotes/quotes/z/zigziglar381984.html

[lx] Tony Robbins. (n.d.). BrainyQuote.com. Retrieved 01 May 2014, from BrainyQuote.com: http://www.brainyquote.com/quotes/quotes/t/tonyrobbin147791.html

[lxi] Maxwell Maltz (n.d.) en.thinkexist.com. Retrieved 07 March 2014 from en.thinkexist.com: http://en.thinkexist.com/quotation/people_who_say_that_life_is_not_worthwhile_are/295009.html

[lxii] Zig Ziglar. (n.d.) Goodreads.com. Retrieved 21 March 2014 from http://www.goodreads.com/quotes/57566-when-obstacles-arise-you-change-your-direction-to-reach-your

[lxiii] Vaclav Havel. (n.d.). Goodreads.com. Retrieved 21 March 2014 from http://www.goodreads.com/quotes/582644-vision-is-not-enough-it-must-be-combined-with-venture

[lxiv] Henri Nouwen. (n.d.). BrainyQuote.com. Retrieved 18 March 2014, from BrainyQuote.com: http://www.brainyquote.com/quotes/quotes/h/henrinouwe588384.html

Accidental Sabbatical

Shari Risoff

Accidental Sabbatical

Shari Risoff

Accidental Sabbatical

Shari Risoff